WRITTEN BY
BOB DUFF & BILL ROOSE

DESIGNED BY
CRAIG C. WHEELER

Copy Editors: Bill Roose and Andrea Nelson
Printed By: Tepel Brothers Printing, Troy, Michigan

All photos were provided by the Lidstrom family; the Detroit Red Wings (Mark Hicks, Christopher Lark, Dan Mannes, Dave Reginek, Dan Ribar, Bill Roose, and Gavin Smith); Detroit Tigers (Mark Cunningham); and Getty Images Photo Service, except where noted. Every reasonable attempt was made to give proper credit. If there is an error, please notify the publisher and a correction will be made in subsequent editions.

Acknowledgements: Sharon Arend, Mark Ernst, Brian Hedger, Greg Innis, Jan Jutbo, Rob Mattina, Kathryn Meredith, Andrea Nelson, Ayron Sequeira, Michaelene Soloway, Dave Reginek, Craig Turnbull, Dave Vote, and Tom Wilson.

Special thanks: Daniel Alfredsson, Red Berenson, Rob Blake, Zdeno Chara, Alex Delvecchio, Marcel Dionne, Patrick Eaves, Viacheslav Fetisov, Danny Gare, Felix Gatt, Doug Gilmour, Danny Grant, Terry Harper, Ted Harris, Victor Hedman, Dennis Hextall, Gordie Howe, Mark Howe, Larry Johnston, Erik Karlsson, Duncan Keith, Red Kelly, Reed Larson, Nick Libett, Jan-Erik Lidstrom, Ted Lindsay, Dan Maloney, Dale McCourt, Lanny McDonald, Jim Nill, Alex Ovechkin, Dennis Polonich, Dominic Raiola, Mickey Redmond, Larry Robinson, Lynn Roose, Borje Salming, Eric Staal, Steven Stamkos, P.K. Subban, Jim Tepel, Errol Thompson, Jonathan Toews, Doug Wilson, Paul Woods, and Henrik Zetterberg.

Very special thanks: Nicklas and Annika Lidstrom, Jimmy Devellano, and Ken Holland.

Printed in the United States of America
Library of Congress Cataloging-in-Publication Data: 2014900782
ISBN: 0-4675-9667-1-9
ISBN 13: 978-1-4675-9667-1

We still remember when we met Nick for the first time. Our director of European scouting Christer Rockstrom wanted us to meet this young lad who was the leading defenseman in his native country of Sweden. A tall, slim and shy 19-year-old teenager showed up in jeans and a polo shirt. His English was not great at the time, but he was able to win us over with his charm. It was apparent to us, that not only was he a talented athlete, he was a person of character. We knew we wanted him to be a part of our team.

Nick is considered one of the top defensemen of his generation and is well known for his durability. He rarely missed a game and he holds many records for his stability. His ability to read the game was uncanny, so he was always in the right place at the right time. His accurate shots from the blue line always amazed us.

Nick's accomplishments are tremendous, yet in spite of them he remains humble. He is a 12-time NHL All Star, seven-time Norris Trophy winner, a Conn Smythe Trophy winner and a four-time Stanley Cup champion. He was named the first European captain of the Red Wings in 2006, and two seasons into his captaincy led his team to the Stanley Cup finals. In 2008, he led the Red Wings to their 11th Stanley Cup, making him the first European captain to lead a team to the Cup.

Like us, the Detroit community fell in love with Nick Lidstrom. There is a street in Novi, Michigan called Nick Lidstrom Drive leading up to the Novi Ice Arena where his four sons played hockey and where Nick never failed to sign autographs for his adoring fans.

We are fortunate that Nick spent his entire 20-season NHL career with the Red Wings, and *"Five: A Salute to Nicklas Lidstrom"* captures many key moments in that wondrous career. That 19-year-old rookie turned into an amazing hockey player and team leader. He was always professional and represented the values that we hold dear – a strong work ethic, commitment, integrity, respect for the fans, love of family, and a willingness to always strive to be the best. Nick and his family will always be in our hearts. We thank Nick for his loyalty to us and wish him and his family the very best as they transition into the next chapter in their lives.

Mike and Marian Ilitch

Owners

Detroit Red Wings

FOREWARD

So it was at the draft, June 17, 1989 at the old Met Center in Minneapolis that head scout Neil Smith and our European scout Christer Rockstrom and then-Western Canada scout Ken Holland presented to me as the general manager a young 19-year-old Swede by the name of Nicklas Lidstrom. Of course, I hadn't seen Nicklas play and so I asked them to describe him as a player. They said that he was a good player with real good hockey sense. They said that he was smooth. Their only concern at that time was they felt that he needed to get significantly stronger. So with that we took him in the third round with the 53rd overall pick.

Of course, at the time none of us realized that he might become the best Red Wings draft pick ever.

I can remember in the 1990s, in Lidstrom's early years, when the NHL Awards show used to be a dinner held in Toronto. I would sit at the Red Wings table with our ownership and management personnel, and of course, Annika and Nick would always be there because, even in the early years he was always a candidate for the Norris Trophy as the NHL's top defenseman.

For three years in a row Nick would be the runner-up for the Norris Trophy. In at least a few of those seasons I was disappointed personally because I certainly felt that Nick should have won the Norris Trophy. However, they couldn't hold him back. He would go on to win the Norris Trophy a magnificent seven times. In his 20-year NHL career he would play in 11 All-Star Games. He was named to 10 First Team All-Star teams, two Second Team All-Star teams.

It is absolutely inarguable that Nick Lidstrom was the greatest defenseman in Detroit Red Wings history.

My first impressions of Nick were that he was quiet and reserved. Over his 20-year career that never changed. He played the game with ease, and he was totally a no-maintenance player from management and the coaching staff. Having Nick Lidstrom for 20 years, our franchise was truly blessed. When Nick retired I wrote him a letter and I said to him, 'Thank you. You've made a few general managers here in Detroit look real good because of your outstanding play.' We feel blessed to have had him for two decades and he was a major cog in four Stanley Cups. Thanks for the memories, Nick, and thank you for being an exceptional role model on and off the ice. I am happy, very happy, that you are remaining in the Red Wings organization.

Jimmy Devellano

Senior Vice President

Detroit Red Wings

I had the pleasure of a "front row" seat for 15 years as the general manager of the Red Wings to watch the greatest defenseman in Red Wings history and one of the greatest defensemen in the history of the National Hockey League.

Nick Lidstrom was the dominant defenseman of his era, and I got to watch him on and off the ice day after day, game after game.

Nick was effortless and made the game look so easy. He had incredible hockey sense and creativity; he was an effortless skater with tremendous agility and mobility and had another gear when he needed it. Nick was poised and patient with the puck, he was a durable player who rarely missed a game over his 20-season career.

Nick played the game like a chess player – he was always a move ahead of his teammates and opponents. He is a major reason why the Red Wings never missed the playoffs in Nick's 20 seasons, and we won 32 playoff rounds, six Presidents' Trophies and four Stanley Cups.

Nick was not only one of the best defensemen in the history of our league but he is also one of the great people in the history of our league. Nick was respectful of everybody in the game: teammates, coaches, opponents, officials, media and fans.

Nick played the game with a gracious spirit and always within the boundaries of the rules. Nick led by example as a player and it was a smooth, natural transition from Stevie Y to Nick as captain of the Red Wings. Furthermore, Nick was the first European captain of a Stanley Cup champion in 2008.

Nick was and is a great role model and ambassador for our team and our league. He is a devoted family man and he and his wife, Annika, are raising four wonderful boys. It's no surprise to me why his teammates called him "The Perfect Human Being".

Ken Holland

Executive Vice President & General Manager
Detroit Red Wings

5 FIVE

Swede Beginnings

A far off dream comes
true for a young
Swedish player

"

He just picked up hockey on his own. I never pushed him harder if you're going to do that and that, no. We have been together with him and watch the hockey game and we've always been there for him but we never pushed him to be better and better. I told Nick to keep the stick on the ice, look up and keep the stick on the ice, that's what I told him to do and he did that.

When Nick was 15 years old I told my wife, 'Nick is going to be the best defenseman in the whole world.' I said so because the coaches here told us he was a very good hockey player, that he going to do very well in the future. I told her that he was going to be the best defenseman in the world and he did it seven times.

"

JAN-ERIK LIDSTROM | Nicklas's Father

This may come as a shock to the system of Detroit Red Wings fans who marveled at his work for two decades on the Detroit defense, but growing up in Vasteras, Sweden, Nicklas Lidstrom worshipped a member of the Toronto Maple Leafs.

Lidstrom was a huge fan of Leafs Hall of Fame defenseman Borje Salming.

"Borje Salming was my big hero growing up," Lidstrom said. "He was a hero, for sure, my idol.

"He was my partner in the Canada Cup in 1991. I had a chance to partner up with him, and that was a big thrill for me."

While Salming was the man, there were other Swedish NHLers on the radar of the young Lidstrom. "I watched Mats Naslund, Hakan Loob, Thomas Steen, Bengt Gustafsson, and guys

Borje Salming, 1991 Canada Cup

that played in the '80s like Ulf Samuelsson and Tomas Sandstrom," Lidstrom said. "There were a lot of players that I followed."

Keeping track of these players wasn't an easy task. With little NHL broadcast in his homeland, Lidstrom resorted to news reports to keep track of his favorite players. "They didn't show any games at all (on TV)," Lidstrom said. "The only games they showed were the Stanley Cup finals, especially if there was a Swede involved. Otherwise, you had to follow it in the newspapers the next day.

"I did follow them, especially the Swedish players. They had their stats in there all the time. Now, with the Internet, which we didn't have back in the '80s, all the kids, all the people back in Sweden are paying attention, and they're good at it."

At a young age, it became apparent that Lidstrom was good at hockey. By the age of 17, he was playing for Vasteras in the Swedish second division. Lidstrom's teammates that

When he came up for the first time with the (Swedish) national team I played with him in the Canada Cup in '91 and we were roommates. He was my defensive partner and shortly after that he went to Detroit and played there. It was fun to really be his roommate and play together and that was almost my second from last (NHL) year and he started his first year and it was great.

He was such an all-arounder, he could do anything. At that time he was 19, of course he was not as good as he was now, but you could see his potential right away that he was going to be good. But of course you can never say he's going to be that good, not like winning the Norris Trophy seven times, never thought of that, and I don't think he did either. But it was fantastic for him.

BORJE SALMING | NHL Defenseman, 1973-90
1996 HOF Inductee

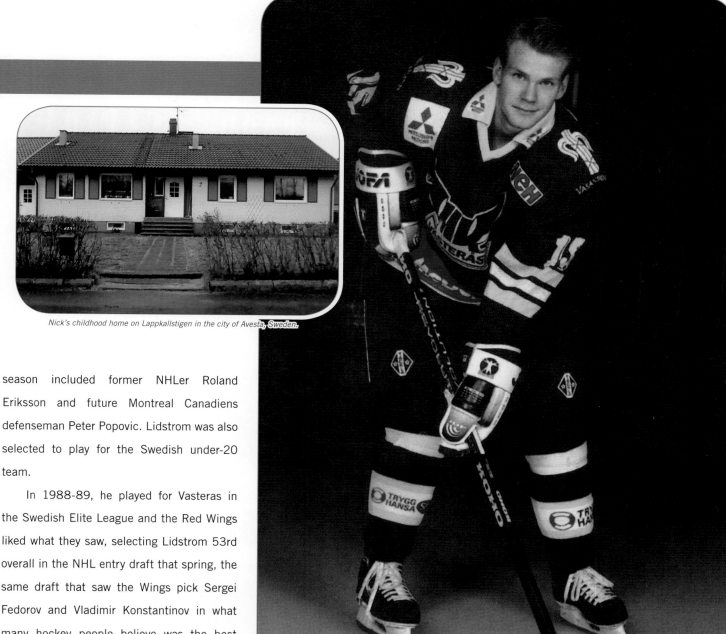

Nick's childhood home on Lappkallstigen in the city of Avesta, Sweden.

season included former NHLer Roland Eriksson and future Montreal Canadiens defenseman Peter Popovic. Lidstrom was also selected to play for the Swedish under-20 team.

In 1988-89, he played for Vasteras in the Swedish Elite League and the Red Wings liked what they saw, selecting Lidstrom 53rd overall in the NHL entry draft that spring, the same draft that saw the Wings pick Sergei Fedorov and Vladimir Konstantinov in what many hockey people believe was the best draft ever conducted by one club.

"Christer Rockstrom deserves most of the credit for that draft," said Neil Smith, Detroit's assistant general manager at the time. "He was the team's European scout and he's the guy who really pushed for Lidstrom, Fedorov and Konstantinov."

Staying with Vasteras for the 1989-90 season, Lidstrom also saw duty with the Swedish national B team and played for the Swedes at the 1990 World Junior Championship in Finland. Lidstrom produced three goals and three assists in seven games, but the all-tournament defensemen were two other future NHLers, Russia's Alexander

Godynyuk and Jiri Slegr of the Czech Republic. The latter would later team with Lidstrom on the 2002 Stanley Cup champion Red Wings.

Lidstrom enjoyed a breakout season in 1990-91, posting 25 points in 38 games for Vasteras, as well as 11 points in 20 games for the Swedish national team, earning a spot on the roster for the World Championship, also played in Finland. Teamed with the likes of Loob, Naslund, Mats Sundin and future Detroit teammate Johan Garpenlov, Lidstrom put up three goals and three assists in 10 games as the Swedes captured the world title.

PLUS+

Lidstrom's son Adam currently plays for VIK Vasteras HK, the same team his dad played for while in Sweden.

1991 LABATT
COUPE CANADA CUP
$6.00

The Red Wings had thoughts of leaving the talented defenseman in Sweden for one more year, but after watching him at those world championships, quickly changed their collective minds.

"They didn't know whether to bring him to North America or not," recalled then-Detroit GM Bryan Murray. "I went over to the world championships to see him. He scored a goal on his first shot and I said, 'Yeah, I think this guy can play.' He was without a doubt the best defenseman on the Swedish national team. Without a doubt. You watched him and you knew there was something good you liked about him.

"He was definitely a key player for Sweden, anchoring the power play — a very good, young, offensive talent. I called (his agent) Don Meehan and we got a deal done."

Lidstrom signed a contract with the Wings on May 19, 1991 and if they needed a little more evidence that he was NHL-ready, it came that fall when Lidstrom suited up for Sweden in the Canada Cup against the best players the NHL had to offer.

Lidstrom formed Sweden's top defensive unit with his boyhood hero Salming in that Canada Cup tournament, where the Swedes lost to eventual champion Canada in the semifinals.

Niklas Lidstrom   *Defense*

"

I couldn't believe how good he was at such a young age. Great skater, great puck-handler; great offensively, great defensively without being a big hitter. He had such great use of his stick. Nobody could beat him one-on-one.

The fact we got him in the third round was amazing.

"

NICK POLANO   Red Wings coach, 1982-85
Assistant GM, 1985-92

In 1992, Nick (far right) and teammate Vladimir Konstantinov (middle) were named to the NHL All-Rookie Team. They were accompanied by eventual teammate, goaltender Dominik Hasek (left).

"I was lucky to play in the Canada Cup," Lidstrom said. "I got used to the small rinks and the NHL style. They dump the puck in a lot, you have to adjust. When they dump it in you have to hold your man up a lot more here than in Europe. You have to read the play.

"That helped me a lot when I first came over here. I got to play six or seven games on smaller ice surfaces here in North America. I'm glad I played in those big tournaments. I met a few NHL players and I got to know how they play.

"I played against Canada and the United States and they had good teams. I played against Russian players, Czechs, Finns. I'd played against most players in the world, so I think I was ready to come over here."

Murray was also impressed by how Lidstrom performed in games against North American opposition in those tourneys, the games that most closely imitated the NHL style.

"I thought he played better against the U.S. and Canada, teams that play the hard-hitting, forechecking game," Murray recalled.

Once he had it in his mind that he was coming to play in the NHL, Lidstrom ramped up the intensity of his off-ice workouts to prepare for the grind of the 80-game NHL slate. He also began to tap into the knowledge of the Swedish NHLers he knew to get the inside scoop on what awaited him.

"When I played in the World championships, I asked Tomas Jonsson, Hakan Loob, Bengt Gustafsson – former NHL players that were playing back in Sweden – how it was over here," Lidstrom said. "I talked to Borje Salming during the Canada Cup. I just tried to talk to as many players as I could.

"I just wanted to know how it is, how the cities are, the food . . . well, everything. They said it was pretty tough the first year to play 80 games. They told me to think of one game at a time. They told me not to worry about

Inside LINE

THE OFFICIAL PUBLICATION OF THE DETROIT RED WINGS

November 1995 $4.00

70th Anniversary

PLUS:
- Meet Bill Evers & Ken Kal
- Fans Catch Merchandise Fever
- Stats, Trivia & More

Whiz Kid
Swift and sleek
NICKLAS LIDSTROM
is at home in Detroit

how I'm going to feel at 40 games or at 60 games and I listened to them."

Upon arrival in Detroit, Lidstrom's tutelage was taken over by Garpenlov, his Swedish teammate.

"When I first came over here, I didn't know anything," Lidstrom said. "How to order a phone, find an apartment – things like that. Johan, he helped me. He was great."

His NHL debut came in hostile surroundings – a 3-3 tie with the Blackhawks at Chicago Stadium. Lidstrom finished the night with a team-high plus-2 and recollects it well.

"I remember being in the old Chicago Stadium," said Lidstrom, who was paired with Brad McCrimmon that night. "The players were telling me it's a loud arena. You're not going to hear anything when you're out there and it was true.

"It was a hard team to play against, the Blackhawks, in the early '90s. They had some real tough teams back then. It was a real tough environment to play in."

Swedish legend Anders Hedberg tabbed Lidstrom as a future NHL star and it didn't take long for evidence of such to emerge. Lidstrom drew two assists in his second NHL game against the Leafs, and then enjoyed a one-goal, two-assist performance in his sixth game, against the St. Louis Blues, scoring his first NHL goal against future teammate Vincent Riendeau.

Just 16 games into his NHL career,

Young Lidstrom was in awe by first NHL defensive partner

Their relationship began in the fall of 1991 at Joe Louis Arena — one, a grizzled veteran of NHL battles, a farm boy from Saskatchewan; the other, a slick Swede from Vasteras who was about to embark on a career as the best defenseman of his generation.

To observers, Brad McCrimmon and Nicklas Lidstrom might have held the appearance of a hockey version of the Odd Couple, but Lidstrom allowed that his view of the partnership was more awed than odd.

"He was my (defensive) partner my first year over here, and he was my roommate, too, so I got to know him really well," Lidstrom recalled of McCrimmon.

Then-Detroit coach-GM Bryan Murray acquired former NHL All-Star McCrimmon from the Calgary Flames, where he'd won a Stanley Cup in 1989, and his veteran presence was a soothing partnership for the learning Lidstrom.

"He was more of a stay-at-home defenseman, and that gave me a chance to be part of the offense," Lidstrom recalled. "He was my partner for every game my first year.

"He was that steady defenseman who stayed home all the time. He would protect me in situations when things got heated. He was a great partner and I learned a lot from him that first year."

Off the ice, the two lived in the same area, so they car pooled to games. Their wives also bonded into a friendship.

"He was always happy, always looking at things the positive way," Lidstrom said. "He was always trying to encourage players when things weren't going their way. He helped me out a lot my first year in the league."

McCrimmon was not surprised by the success of his new teammate.

"You take an 18-year-old underage draft and throw him in the National Hockey League, he's pretty raw," McCrimmon said in a 1992 interview. "He'd have to be an exceptional player to do well.

"With Nick, I think having been exposed to the World Championships, the Canada Cup and five years of the Swedish Elite League, he's had good experience.

"He's a good solid player in every aspect. He doesn't do any one thing outstanding, but at the same time he has no weaknesses. He's solid both offensively and defensively. He's got good composure and he works hard. He's a great skater. You can't say that he has one dominating quality.

"Yes, he's a good skater, but you can't just describe him as a great skater. Yes, he's a good puckhandler, but you can't say he's just a good puckhandler. He's solid in all the skills and he's a solid positional player."

Red Wings senior vice president Jimmy Devellano remembers how seamlessly the pairing blended together.

"Nick was a rookie from Sweden and Brad was his first playing partner," Devellano said. "He upgraded our defense and sort of got Lidstrom broken in as a young Swede coming over from Europe.

"Lidstrom understood that it was nice to have a veteran NHL player that knew the ropes and that made Lidstrom's transition into the league a very good one. As you know, he never looked back."

Traded to the Hartford Whalers in 1993, McCrimmon would return to the Detroit organization in 2008 as an assistant to coach Mike Babcock. In 2011, McCrimmon accepted a head-coaching position with Lokomotiv Yaroslavl of Russia's Kontinental Hockey League and gave his life pursuing the game he loved.

McCrimmon was among 43 killed when the team plane crashed shortly after takeoff en route to the club's season opener on Sept. 7 , 2011.

"He wanted to be a head coach," Lidstrom said. "He wanted to see what it would be like, being a head coach in Russia.

"We all wished him well when we heard the news."

Lidstrom collected four points in a game against the Blues, a total that would stand as his career single-game high. His 49 assists were a new rookie mark for a Detroit defenseman and tied Marcel Dionne for the overall Red Wings rookie standard. Lidstrom's 60 points equaled Reed Larson's team record for rookie defenders.

"He played tremendously," Murray recalled. "Nicklas was one of our key people all season. I played him and Brad McCrimmon against the opposition's best line and his plus/minus showed he didn't give up a lot. He moved the puck and got us out of trouble a lot. He was an important player on the point for us. He killed penalties. He played all the time."

Lidstrom finished third in the NHL with a plus-36 rating that led all rookies. He also topped NHL rookies in assists. He was named to the NHL's All-Rookie Team and finished second to Vancouver's Pavel Bure in Calder Trophy voting.

Looking back, Lidstrom remembers his hopes for that first season with the Red Wings weren't nearly as grandiose.

"My goal was to make the team and then play as many games as I could," Lidstrom said. "I was really surprised I did that well. I didn't play on that good of a team in Sweden, but here I was, playing the power play and picking up a lot of points (with the Red Wings)."

Lidstrom also chuckled at what course his life might have taken were he not to cross the Atlantic Ocean and become a Red Wing.

"I finished school in Sweden when I was 20 to become an engineer, but I didn't fulfill the course because I came here instead," he said. "If I stayed in Sweden and did more studying, I would've become an engineer.

"I like the decision I made."

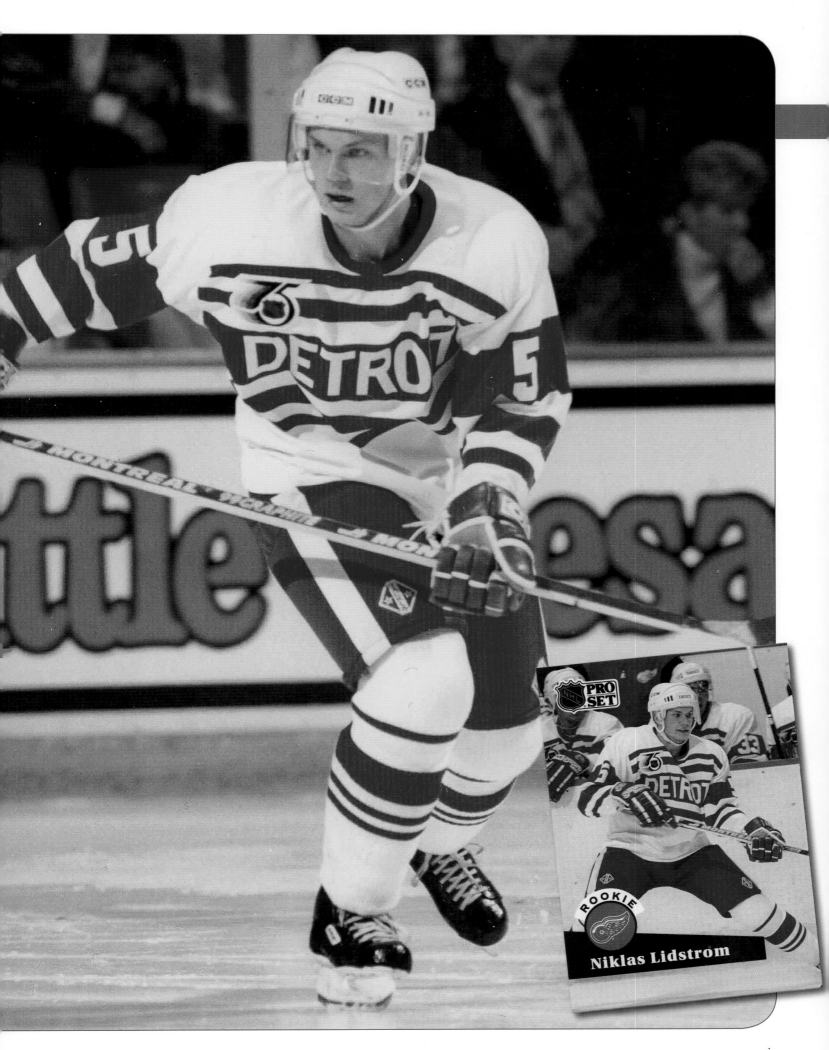

ROOKIE

Niklas Lidström

5 FIVE

Red Wings Revival

Lidstrom's arrival helped
launch Detroit's rise to
NHL powerhouse

Every company has an employee like Nicklas Lidstrom. The person who shows up on time each day, always works hard and gets the job done quietly, yet efficiently. Doesn't complain, never seeks attention and seldom receives any.

Long before the rest of the hockey world caught on, the Red Wings had already figured out the underscored value of Lidstrom's solidly effective game.

"He was the most important player on our team," former Detroit captain Steve Yzerman said. "We'd known that he was great all along. He was very quiet and on the ice he didn't have the flash of a Brian Leetch or was going to dash end-to-end and score beautiful goals.

"He wasn't going to land big open-ice checks, but he'd get in front of the guys and didn't get knocked off the puck. He did everything well, just not with a lot of flash. He was very efficient and played a quiet game."

Seeing Lidstrom in action night after night, the Wings were able to comprehend his importance to their scheme as they climbed the ladder to become a legitimate Stanley Cup contender by the mid-1990s.

It was so nice to come to the game and know that Nick was playing because you knew everything was taken care of. You knew he was going to play well, he probably wasn't going to get hurt, he was going to play big minutes, he was going to play against the other team's best players and you had a chance of winning when he was in the lineup which was all the time.

I still remember when we played Philly in the finals that year, I think we had Jamie Macoun, Slava Fetisov and Bob Rouse, big strong guys. We were down talking to Scotty Bowman and thinking, 'OK, how are we going to match up against Eric Lindros and the Legion of Doom?' He said, 'I'm going to use Lidstrom and Murphy.' We said, 'Lidstrom and Murphy? Murphy's slow supposedly and Lidstrom's not very strong.' We thought, 'Are you crazy?' But Scotty was right, he put them out there and the Legion of Doom never touched the puck. They got frustrated and we won four straight. So that just shows you how good Nick was. You couldn't hit him and he was always thinking one step ahead of you.

JIM NILL NHL Right Wing, 1981-90
Red Wings Executive, 1993-2013

"He did everything really well," former teammate Brendan Shanahan said. "If you watched him closely, you really appreciated how good he was handling the puck, passing, positioning himself. He was just great all around."

It's no coincidence that Detroit's run of playoff appearances, which started the season before Lidstrom arrived, continued unabated through his 20-season career, as he tied an NHL postseason record for most years consecutively in the Stanley Cup playoffs, a mark he shares with another legendary defenseman, Larry Robinson.

Wings fans probably don't want to think about how close it came to never happening.

The sophomore jinx took hold of Lidstrom during the 1992-93 campaign. He endured a 48-game goalless drought and finished the season with 41 points, 19 fewer than during his rookie year.

"I thought it would be like the first year, but I struggled and I stopped getting involved offensively," Lidstrom recalled of his second NHL season.

There was speculation that the Wings would package Lidstrom in a deal to acquire the rights to power forward Eric Lindros, the top pick in the 1991 NHL entry draft who'd refused to report to the Quebec Nordiques.

This was one deal that the Wings were glad they never made.

NICKLAS LIDSTROM

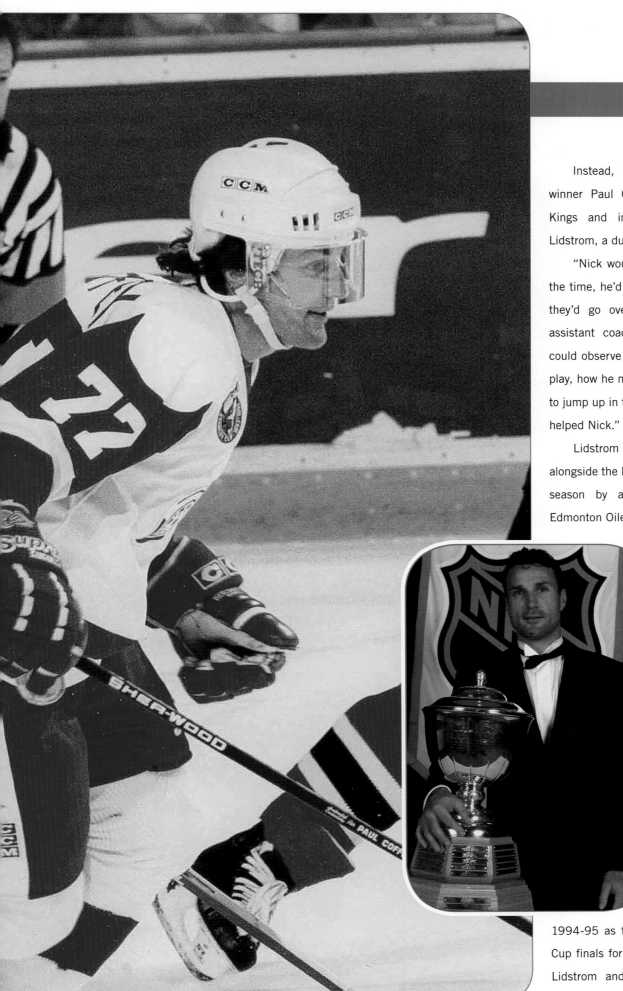

Instead, they acquired Norris Trophy winner Paul Coffey from the Los Angeles Kings and immediately paired him with Lidstrom, a duo that instantly paid dividends.

"Nick would be on the ice with Paul all the time, he'd be on the bench with him and they'd go over situations," former Detroit assistant coach Dave Lewis recalled. "He could observe how Paul played on the power play, how he moved the puck and knew when to jump up in the play – all these things really helped Nick."

Lidstrom reaped the benefits of skating alongside the NHL record holder for goals in a season by a defenseman (48 with the Edmonton Oilers in 1985-86).

"Playing with Paul was a really good learning experience for me," Lidstrom said. "Just watching him was a great experience. He never stopped skating. I felt pretty lucky because I was paired with Borje Salming in the (1991) Canada Cup, so that made two great defensemen I'd played with."

Coffey won the Norris Trophy in 1994-95 as the Wings reached the Stanley Cup finals for the first time since 1966 with Lidstrom and Coffey skating as their top defensive tandem.

MR. UNPREDICTABLE

"It was a warm-up in Detroit at The Joe and I was skating by him in warm-up. I stopped to stretch at center ice and he says, 'Hey, I follow you on Twitter.' I was kind of shocked that he even has Twitter or knew what it was. It was pretty much my most epic moment of my career."

PAUL "BIZNASTY" BISSONNETTE
Phoenix Coyotes Winger

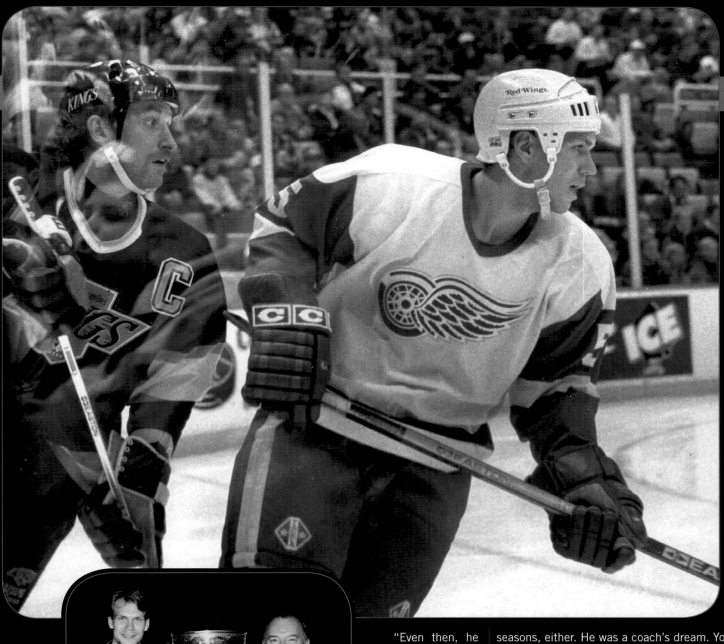

"Even then, he was a quiet student of the game," Coffey said of Lidstrom. "Even at 22, when I first saw him, he had dignity and class. He made the game look easy and it was like that from Day 1. He had the perfect mind for it and the perfect frame. He was a rare breed, a bigger guy who could play and move.

"His consistency was the thing that made him who he was. There were never any 100-point seasons, but there were no crappy seasons, either. He was a coach's dream. You knew what you were going to get every shift, every game."

Durability was another Lidstrom trademark. He played every game in seven of his 20 NHL seasons and missed only one or two games in eight other seasons, playing 1,564 of a possible 1,608 regular-season games and 263 of 265 in the playoffs. In Stanley Cup history, only one other skater – former teammate Chris Chelios (266) – played more postseason games.

"He made so few mistakes," former Detroit coach Scotty Bowman said. "Where could you ever see a player who would miss so few games, who could play at his level?"

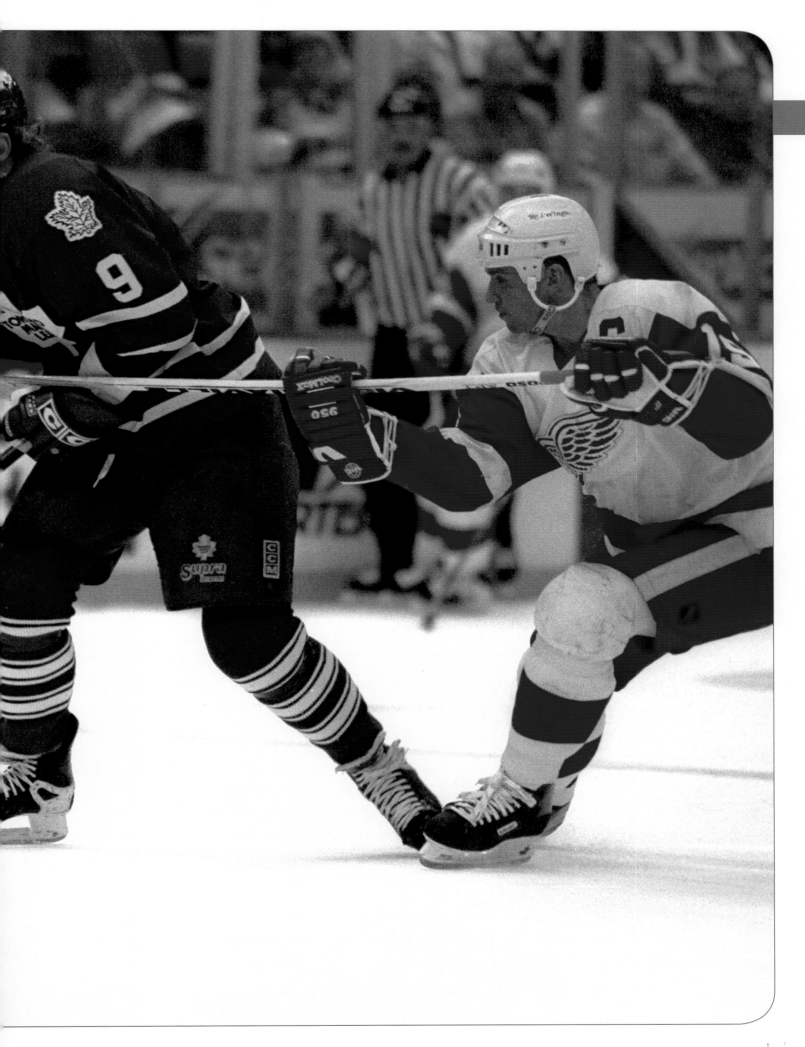

"

When I first met him you could see that he had a lot of potential. Nick was calm, poised and didn't make mistakes. You knew he was going to be good, and I think he's one of the top three or four defensemen that ever played the game.

There used to be the cartoon character 'Go Go Gadget' and I used to say that Nick had 'Go Go Gadget' arms, I mean, guys would get 7-8 feet away because they knew against certain defensemen they could get in tighter and all of a sudden the arm would come out and 'Boom!' the puck was gone and going the other way. And then his hand-eye coordination was just phenomenal. Any puck that came his way, whether it was a saucer pass or whatever, he generally was able to knock it out of the air. There were so many things he could do.

But as a person, he was just a very nice, quiet, unassuming guy. He was just agreeable with anything, just very respectful of his peers and of the media. I think you'd have an awful time trying to find one person to say one bad thing about Nick Lidstrom and his character.

"

| MARK HOWE | NHL Defenseman, 1979-95 Red Wings Teammate, 1992-95 |

Lidstrom's shot helped Red Wings 'bounce' back in 2002

Faced with an uphill battle in their 2002 opening-round series against the No. 8 seed Canucks, the Red Wings received a fortuitous bounce from Nicklas Lidstrom.

Trailing the series two games to none, the Red Wings' playoff hopes were on life-support as the series shifted to scenic Vancouver.

"We thought at the time that we had a grasp on the series," said Todd Bertuzzi, who played in Vancouver from 1997-2006. "But they had Hall-of-Famers and guys who had done it, and we were kind of the new kids on the block, young and inexperienced, and we paid the price for that inexperience.

"When Nick scored that goal from center ice that was kind of the icing on the cake, which led them to stealing the series."

Canucks goalie Dan Cloutier whiffed on Lidstrom's 100-foot slap shot from center ice in the waning seconds of the second period in Game 3.

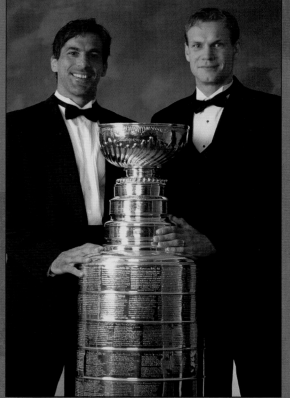

Even the best teams in the world need breaks every now and then, and the Red Wings took full advantage of Lidstrom's bomb that gave them a 2-1 lead and enough energy to flip the tables on the Canucks, who never recovered from the long-distance shot.

"That was the turnaround in that series, it's tough to see it any other way," Red Wings forward Tomas Holmstrom said. "After that goal, Coultier wasn't really sure how he was going to stop the next puck, because you let one of those in and they knew we got to him."

The scoring play couldn't have come at a better time for the visitors. Lidstrom's goal came moments after the Red Wings killed off a Vancouver 5-on-3 advantage that lasted 47-seconds. But the Canucks failed to score and Lidstrom quieted the towel-waving sellout crowd at GM Place, and zapped any momentum they had going at the time.

"We were feeling confident in the second, especially after killing off those penalties and getting a goal on top of that was huge," Lidstrom told the media after the game. "That's playoff hockey, that's what happens in the playoffs and you just have to bounce back if it happens against you and try to make a break for yourself."

Bertuzzi scored the Canucks' lone goal in Game 3, but he couldn't convert a penalty shot that would have tied the score in the third period after Lidstrom dragged him down on a breakaway.

Lidstrom's skills and his ability to avoid big hits throughout his career frustrated physically intimidating guys like Bertuzzi, who never could get a clean body check on the Red Wings' defenseman.

"He's just one of those guys that you couldn't hit, and I tried for a while," Bertuzzi said. "I finally got over it because you just don't want to hit him. He's that big of a deal and I had that much respect for him that there was no point in me going out of my way to do something even though I couldn't ever get him if I tried."

The Red Wings finished with a 3-1 win in Game 3 and won the next three games to advance to the conference semifinals against the St. Louis Blues.

By July, Lidstrom had won his third Stanley Cup, as well as his second Norris Trophy, as the league's best defenseman.

"My fondest memory is sitting with Nick at the (2002) awards banquet," Hall-of-Fame defenseman Chris Chelios said. "We were loaded, that team. To finish it off like we did, with the start we had (down 0-2 to Vancouver), was too good to be true. One of the highlights of my career was sitting with my wife, his wife and being runner up to Nick Lidstrom. I'll never forget that moment. I was in disbelief I was sitting next to Nick after winning the Cup. That was the dream year, perfect year. Couldn't top that."

Not to mention doing so while playing the toughest position on the ice in terms of physical battles and split-second decisions, and while frequently skating upwards of 30 minutes per game.

"During the game, you're into the game so much, you don't realize how much you are playing," Lidstrom said of the ice time he'd play. "It's not something I really thought about much. I'd just go out there and play."

For one of the rare times during his early NHL career, Lidstrom found himself in the national spotlight the night of June 1, 1995. That night at Joe Louis Arena, he scored on Chicago's Ed Belfour 1:01 into overtime to give Detroit a 2-1 decision over the Blackhawks in the opening game of the Western Conference finals. It was the first Stanley Cup overtime goal scored by a Red Wings player in a game at Detroit since Jerry Melnyk scored against Toronto at Olympia Stadium on March 27, 1960.

"Nick didn't do any one thing awesome, but he did everything great," Coffey said.

Former NHL coach Paul Maurice added, "He had so much patience and such an outstanding level of skill. And it didn't matter what type of game it was – hard-hitting, high skill, grinding – his game never changed. He had tremendous tempo out there."

Those inside the game were catching on to the subtle greatness of Lidstrom and soon, the entire hockey world would be let in on the secret. **5**

LEADER

Nicklas Lidstrom

5 FIVE

Mr. Norris

Lidstrom makes NHL's
award for top defenseman
his personal property

In the spring of 1998, as the Red Wings were in the midst of defending the Stanley Cup title they'd won the year before, the National Hockey League finally recognized the quiet superstar working within their midst. For the first time in his career, Nicklas Lidstrom was announced as a Norris Trophy finalist.

"Unofficially, we all kind of expected it," Detroit forward Brent Gilchrist said.

"It had been a long time coming," added Detroit winger Darren McCarty. "He's always been the most underrated player in the league – our little secret."

The secret was out. Though it would still be some time until Lidstrom won the award as the NHL's best defenseman – he was runner-up to Rob Blake in 1997-98, Al MacInnis in 1998-99 and Chris Pronger in 1999-2000 – everyone knew it was merely a matter of time until he ascended to his rightful place atop the heap of NHL defenders.

"I'm sure he was happy to accept the award, but I don't think the drive for him was to win it," said Larry Murphy, Lidstrom's former defense partner. "The drive for him was to just play well."

Even opponents nodded to the greatness of Lidstrom. "It's amazing that he didn't get the Norris Trophy last season," Toronto Maple Leafs captain Mats Sundin said during the 1998-99 season. "Lidstrom has been Detroit's dominating player during the two consecutive years they have won the Stanley Cup."

"

I loved played against him, and kind of idolizing him and being able to watch him and learn from him. I had game tape broken down on Nick Lidstrom to see how he played just to try and understand how effective he was and why he was that effective. It's a simple equation: he didn't do a lot of movement on the ice; he was in the right spot all of the time, but it's hard to duplicate.

When we met in the playoffs in 2010 when I was in San Jose, I knew I was done and I figured he had a few more years, though I wasn't sure how many more. For me, I remember that handshake was more like a thank you. It was great watching you for 20 years, and now I'm going to step aside. It was that kind of handshake, which was different than any other we ever had. … For me, he's the best player that I've ever seen play defense.

"

ROB BLAKE | NHL Defenseman, 1989-2010
Norris Trophy Recipient, 1998

During his acceptance speech following his inaugural Norris Trophy win in 2001, one of the first people Lidstrom thanked was Brad McCrimmon, his first defensive partner in Detroit.

For his part, Lidstrom seemed unconcerned by the lack of individual love being thrown his way.

"I always looked at the Norris as a bonus," Lidstrom said. "It's an honor to be a finalist. I thought winning it would be great, but the No. 1 thing was to win the Stanley Cup.

"The Stanley Cup is the goal you set at the start of the season and it's the goal you work toward as a team. The individual awards are a bonus that you win because you had a good, solid year."

As the 2000-01 season got underway, there was a sense that Lidstrom's time to shine had finally arrived.

"Nick Lidstrom deserves to win this year," suggested NHL analyst Brian Engblom, a former NHL defenseman. "It's funny how it works. With a lot of the awards, you have to be

around for a couple of years to get acknowledged. Rob Blake went through that."

St. Louis Blues coach Ken Hitchcock remembered how Lidstrom's stock rose among NHL players. "A number of guys put him down not only as best defenseman but also as the NHL's most valuable player," he said. "That's how highly he was regarded."

Perhaps what held Lidstrom back the most was that he wasn't one to brag, and since his game was more about simple, stalwart play, highlight packages rarely featured footage of his on-ice performances.

"Nick didn't seek out the spotlight and the spotlight doesn't usually shine on guys like him," Murphy said. "Guys who can go end-to-end with the puck, like Brian Leetch, or big hitters like Scott Stevens, they get noticed.

Nick brought his 2002 hockey hardware to his parents' cottage in Sweden where he shared the Norris Trophy, Stanley Cup and Conn Smythe Trophy with his family. From left to right are sisters Ann-Sofie and Eva-Lena, his mom Gerd, dad Jan-Erik, and sister Petra.

FIVE

I was fortunate to play with some of the greatest defensemen. I had Bobby Orr the last year that he played here in Chicago. He was my idol as a defenseman. Larry Robinson in the Canada Cup. I mean, those were two of the greatest. Nicky is different than both of those two in his own way. Every little play he made, you'd sit there and go, 'Wow, he made that play look that easy,' because he'd already processed the information and made the play. And it happened time after time after time.

He could still be playing today, there's no doubt because of the way he thinks the game. But I think the other thing about him is he would do what was needed at whatever time of the game it was. It was just to make a great play, create some offense or snuff a play out for the PK or knowing the clock and the time, he thought the game at a different level, maybe, than any other defenseman during that era he was playing.

DOUG WILSON | NHL Defenseman, 1977-93
Norris Trophy Recipient, 1982

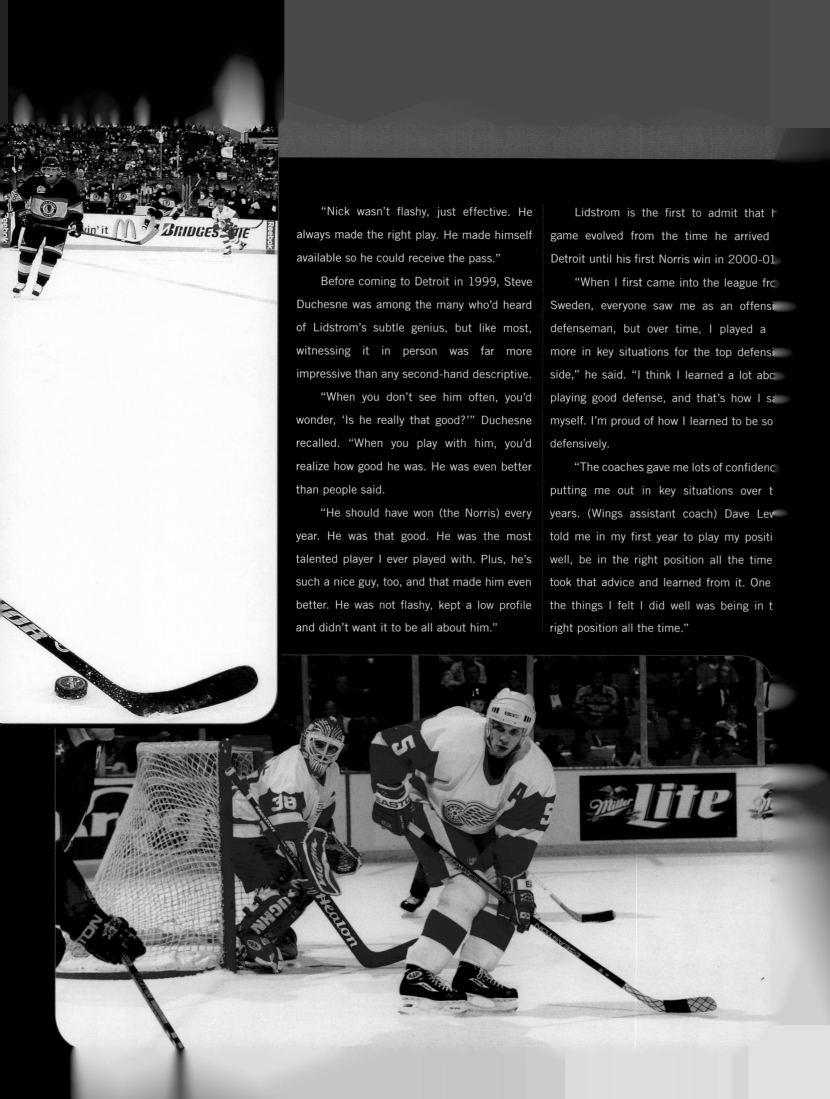

"Nick wasn't flashy, just effective. He always made the right play. He made himself available so he could receive the pass."

Before coming to Detroit in 1999, Steve Duchesne was among the many who'd heard of Lidstrom's subtle genius, but like most, witnessing it in person was far more impressive than any second-hand descriptive.

"When you don't see him often, you'd wonder, 'Is he really that good?'" Duchesne recalled. "When you play with him, you'd realize how good he was. He was even better than people said.

"He should have won (the Norris) every year. He was that good. He was the most talented player I ever played with. Plus, he's such a nice guy, too, and that made him even better. He was not flashy, kept a low profile and didn't want it to be all about him."

Lidstrom is the first to admit that h game evolved from the time he arrived Detroit until his first Norris win in 2000-01

"When I first came into the league fro Sweden, everyone saw me as an offensi defenseman, but over time, I played a more in key situations for the top defensi side," he said. "I think I learned a lot abo playing good defense, and that's how I sa myself. I'm proud of how I learned to be so defensively.

"The coaches gave me lots of confidenc putting me out in key situations over t years. (Wings assistant coach) Dave Lev told me in my first year to play my positi well, be in the right position all the time took that advice and learned from it. One the things I felt I did well was being in t right position all the time."

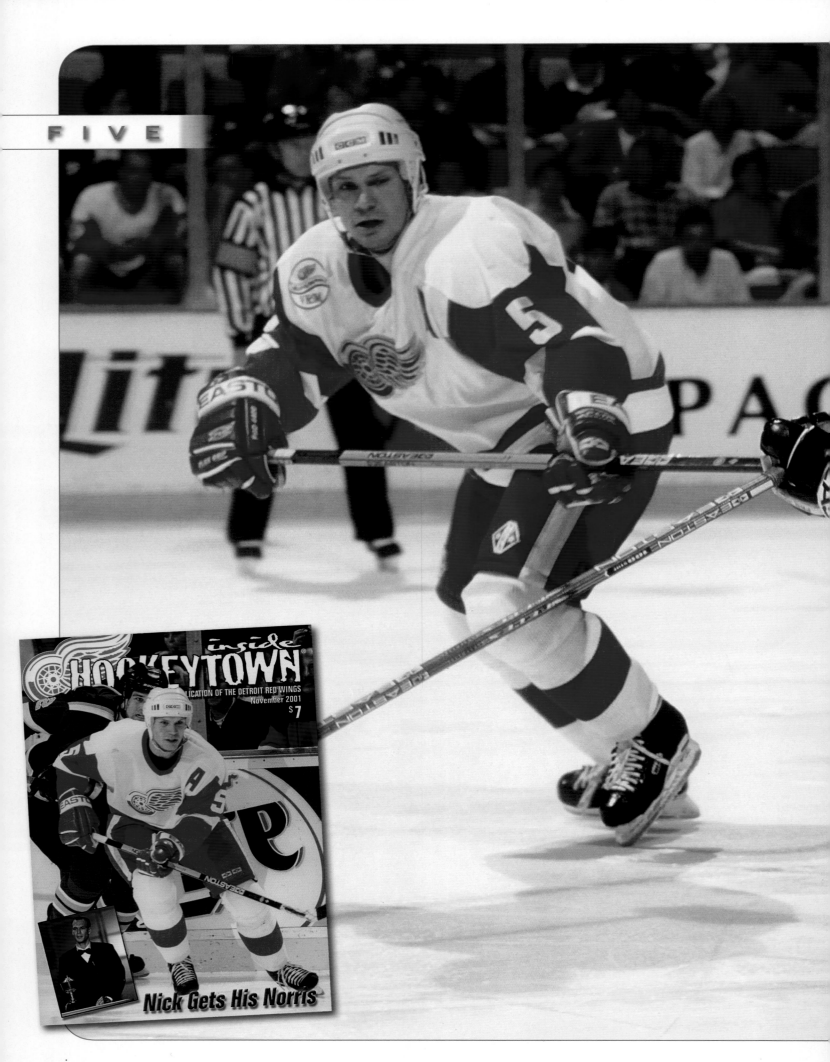

inside
HOCKEYTOWN
LICATION OF THE DETROIT RED WINGS
November 2001
$7

Nick Gets His Norris

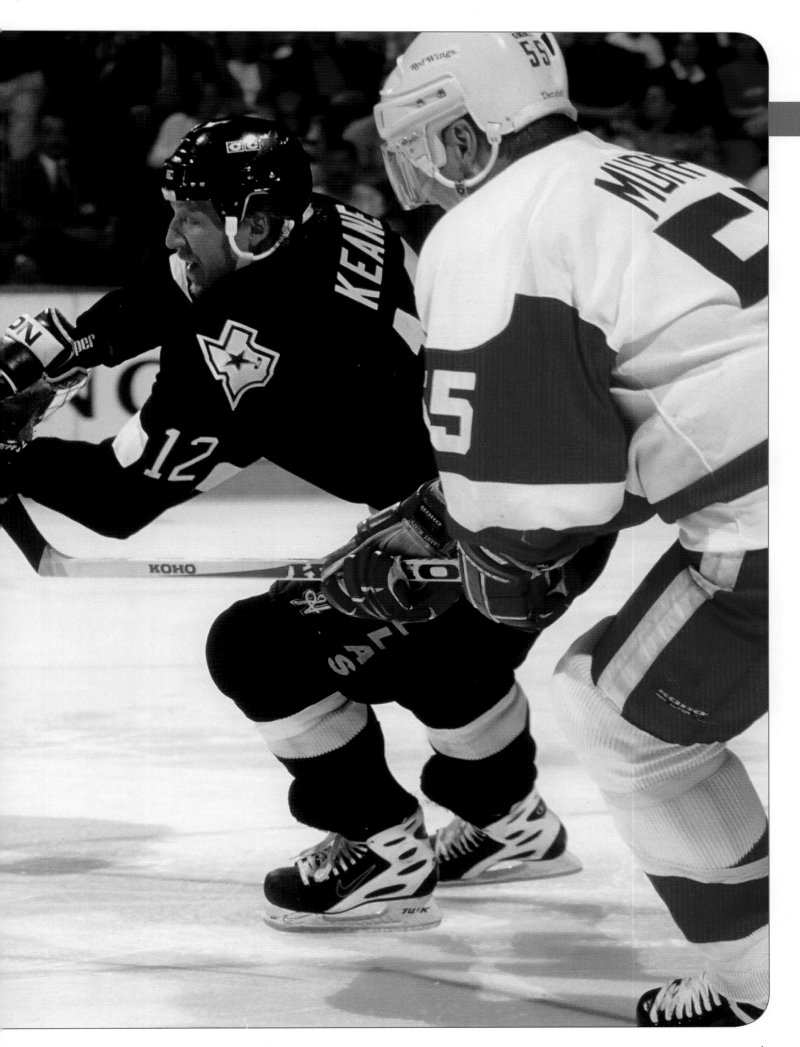

+PLUS

Lidstrom was blunt and to the point when he wasn't voted a Norris finalist in 2003-04. "I didn't have a strong enough year to be nominated," he said. "And that's pretty much the bottom line. I wish I would have played better throughout the year."

Once his name went on the Norris for the first time, Lidstrom owned the trophy as if it were his personal property. He won again in 2001-02 and 2002-03, joining Doug Harvey, Bobby Orr and Pierre Pilote as the only defensemen to win the Norris in three successive seasons. Just for good measure, Lidstrom turned another Norris hat-trick from 2005-06 through 2007-08. He won his seventh Norris in 2010-11. At the age of 41, Lidstrom became the oldest Norris winner, joining Harvey with seven wins, one shy of Orr's record eight Norris Trophies.

"I certainly don't compare myself to Bobby Orr," Lidstrom said of the Boston Bruins legend. "He's someone I'd like to take a picture with."

Others were more than willing to place Lidstrom up among the game's elite rearguards.

"I don't know what else you say," said Hall of Famer Scott Niedermayer, the 2003-04 Norris winner. "He was recognized a number of times for good reason, because he was a very, very good defenseman, a smart player with great skills, and a good leader. He was everything that you needed to be in his situation.

"It's tough to say there was anybody better."

Those charged with the task of getting past Lidstrom to the Detroit net shuddered at the notion of deciphering the code that could break him.

"To me, he was the hardest defenseman to play against in the game," former Colorado Avalanche captain Joe Sakic said. "He was the best in the game. It was just his hockey sense – his smarts, he was always in the right spot – it was almost like he knew what you're going to do before you did.

"

To me, he epitomizes what a Norris Trophy winner should be. He was a great player in both ends of the rink, played in all situations and, of course, had great longevity. … Just having seen him, the way he sees the ice, the way he controls the play, great shot. He always had his shot on net and was a great passer. He had a great hockey mind, for sure.

Winning the Norris seven times, that's always a discussion that people have every year, you know, 'Did he win it because he had the most points or did he win it because he was one of the better players?' That's a question that everybody asks all the time, but he was certainly deserving of it. And to win his last one in his 40s, that's pretty impressive, when you're that age and you can still be noted as one of the best in the league, he certainly doesn't take a backseat to anybody.

"

LARRY ROBINSON NHL Defenseman, 1972-92
Norris Trophy Recipient, 1977, 1980

Nominated six times for the award, Lady Byng eluded Lidstrom

When they talked about Nicklas Lidstrom as a candidate for the Lady Byng Trophy as the NHL's best combination of ability and sportsmanship, back in Sweden, his family would laugh.

"People have told me that I'm unflappable, but my parents used to tell me I was wild until I was five years old," said Lidstrom, though he couldn't even recall ever receiving a detention while in school.

Six times, Lidstrom was a finalist for the Lady Byng, a record for a defenseman, though he never won the award. He was runner-up in the voting in 1998-99, 1999-2000, 2000-01, 2002-03 and 2010-11 and finished third in the balloting in 2001-02.

"It would have been such an honor to win the Byng," he said.

Five times during his 20-season career, Lidstrom garnered less than 20 minutes in penalties, and in three other seasons was assessed exactly 20 minutes, astonishing for someone playing his position, because the nature of defense is that a player is frequently required to engage in one-on-one physical battles with opponents.

"It had a lot to do with my positioning," Lidstrom said of his lack of penalty minutes. "I try to be in the right spot all the time and not get beat to the outside."

That sentiment was echoed by those who coached Lidstrom. "He was such a good positional player that he rarely had to take penalties," said ex-Detroit coach Dave Lewis, a former NHL defenseman.

"Defensemen use their stick more than most players. Usually, when a defenseman gets penalties, it's because of his stick — you cross-check someone at the net, you get beat and give the guy a tug. Since he rarely got beat, he didn't have to rely on that."

Prior to Lidstrom's six nominations, the only defensemen to win the award were both Red Wings — Bill Quackenbush in 1948-49 and Red Kelly in

1950-51, 1952-53 and 1953-54. In 2011-12, Bryan Campbell of the Florida Panthers became the third defenseman to win the Lady Byng.

Kelly, who also won the Lady Byng playing center for the Toronto Maple Leafs in 1960-61, thinks people have a misconception of what the award stands for.

"I never thought of the Lady Byng being about penalty minutes," Kelly explained. "People look at the penalty minutes aspect, but to me, it's an award which goes to a player who displays sportsmanship.

"Don't tell me about (Lidstrom's) penalty minutes. Tell me how many goals were scored against the team when he was on the ice. I'll bet it wasn't too many. That's what mattered — not that he didn't get penalties, but that he didn't get penalties and still got the job done."

That's the epitome of what Lidstrom's game was all about.

"Nick is the guy," Red Wings general manager Ken Holland said. "He was a pro's pro."

PLUS

In 2001-02, Lidstrom and Chris Chelios were both nominated as Norris Trophy finalists. "We were hoping for a tie," said Lidstrom, who ultimately won. They were also named to the NHL First All-Star Team, the first time teammates had filled both defense positions since 1947-48, when Detroit's (Black) Jack Stewart and Bill Quackenbush were the players.

"He wasn't flashy on the ice, but he'd play 30, 35 minutes a game and do everything well. You'd see Lidstrom on the ice and you knew you're going to have a tough night."

Amazingly, Lidstrom put up these impressive Norris totals even though his first win didn't come until after his 31st birthday. Orr and Harvey were both 21 when they captured their first Norris Trophy.

Lidstrom smiles when he ponders his place in history. "I probably would have laughed right in their face," he said of the thought of anyone suggesting he might win the Norris seven times when he first arrived in Detroit back in 1991. "I would have been

honored just to get one. This is really something I'm proud of – to have been able to be nominated for so many years and able to win the Norris seven times. It's been a great honor for me."

As for his favorite Norris memory, that one might catch you by surprise. It was the low-cut Toronto Maple Leafs jersey dress worn by actress Tia Carrere when she presented Lidstrom the Norris at the 2001 NHL Awards.

"I remember Tia Carrere being the presenter with the Norris the first time I won it," Lidstrom said. "That sticks out." **5**

"

When it comes down to winning seven times Norris Trophy, being nominated nine of 10 times, just being nominated that many times for being on top of the league as far as top defenseman for that long, it's unbelievable. I've been nominated five times and that's only half of what he was. It just happened that I only won once; he won seven times.

I'm not sure which All-Star game that was but I was standing next to him and I said 'Hey you're an unbelievable player, I'm always watching you play and I admire the way you play and it's an honor.' And he said, 'Really?' That was a question. I'm like, 'Oh my God this guy is one of the best and he's so humble.' I was like, 'Wow, that's pretty amazing.'

"

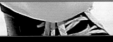

| ZDENO CHARA | Boston Bruins Defenseman
Norris Trophy Recipient, 2009 |

5 FIVE

International Man of History

Lidstrom rewrote the NHL record book for European players

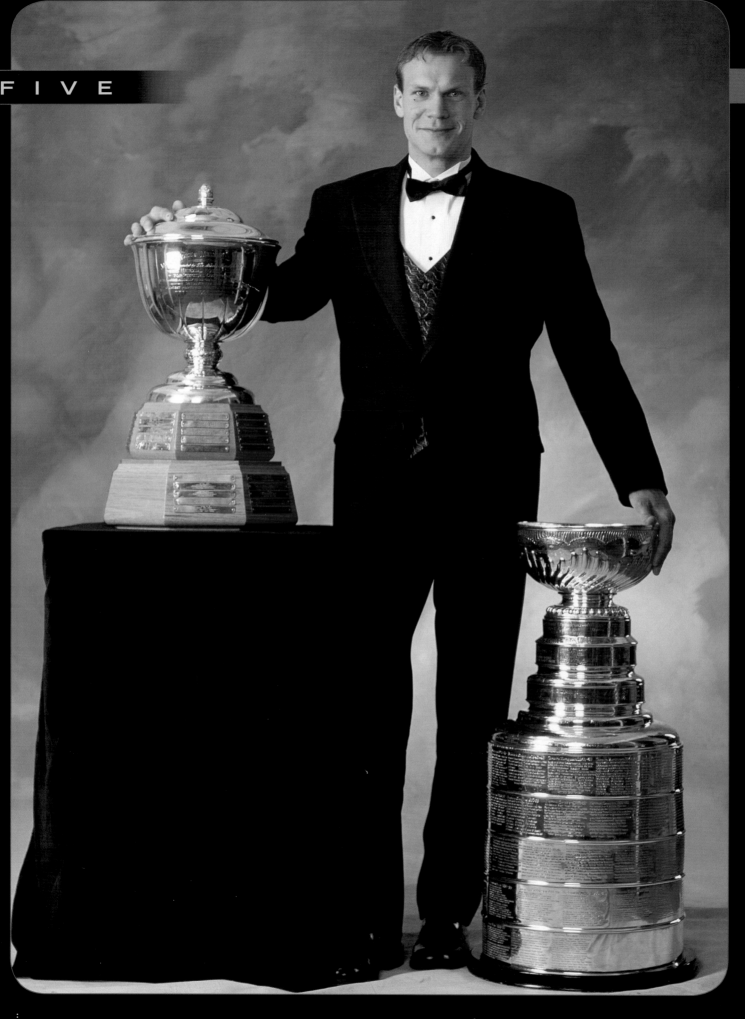

Before Nicklas Lidstrom, European players had led the NHL in scoring, and been chosen the MVP and the rookie of the year. They'd been selected first overall in the entry draft. Then Lidstrom came along and broke through all the remaining barriers facing the NHL's vastly skilled group of European talent.

In 2000-01, Lidstrom became the first European to win the Norris Trophy as the league's best defenseman. "I don't really know why," Lidstrom said, trying to rationalize how he could be the first to win the award. "I think there's been some great European defensemen over the years, (Viacheslav) Fetisov being one of them, and Borje Salming in the `70s and `80s."

The following season, after the Red Wings stopped the Carolina Hurricanes in the Stanley Cup finals, Lidstrom was awarded the Conn Smythe Trophy as playoff MVP, also a first for a European player. "I feel very good about that," Lidstrom said. "It's a significant honor. I think it makes it even sweeter being the first European."

Six years later, when the Wings again captured Lord Stanley's mug, it was Lidstrom who accepted the trophy from NHL commissioner Gary Bettman as the first European-born and trained captain of a Stanley Cup champion.

"It felt great being the first guy to touch the Cup on our team," Lidstrom said. "Otherwise, it felt the same as winning the previous ones, where you're so happy with the end result. You start training camp with a goal, and that is to win the Stanley Cup."

None of it – the Norris, the Conn Smythe, the Stanley Cup – likely would have ever come Lidstrom's way had it not been for the hockey groundwork that he laid in his native land. If it weren't for Sweden, Lidstrom might never have become a Red Wing.

In the spring of 1991, as he weighed the decision whether to accept an offer from the Red Wings to play in the NHL, for the first time in his career, Lidstrom was picked to the Swedish team headed to the IIHF World Championships.

When it was all over, Lidstrom had turned in a stellar performance as the Swedes captured the world title for just the second time since 1962. "That was my first experience with the national team at the highest level," he said.

"Of course, winning a gold medal in my first big tournament was huge for me at that point in my career. I just got an offer from the Wings to come over and play for Detroit and that was a fairly big tournament for me to kind of showcase myself. Then on top of that, winning the gold medal was huge and a big stepping stone for me in my career."

Lidstrom signed with the Red Wings shortly after the tournament and that fall, played for the Swedish team – known as Tre Kronor for the three crowns on the front of the jersey – once more against the NHL's best in the Canada Cup.

"I grew up watching all of the different world championships and the Olympics because every kid in Sweden dreams of playing for the national team one day," Lidstrom said. "I was one of those kids.

"I wanted to play for Team Sweden and I finally had a chance to do that when I put on that national team jersey. It's a special feeling. You feel very proud, especially when you're representing your country. To be able to do that was a big thrill for me."

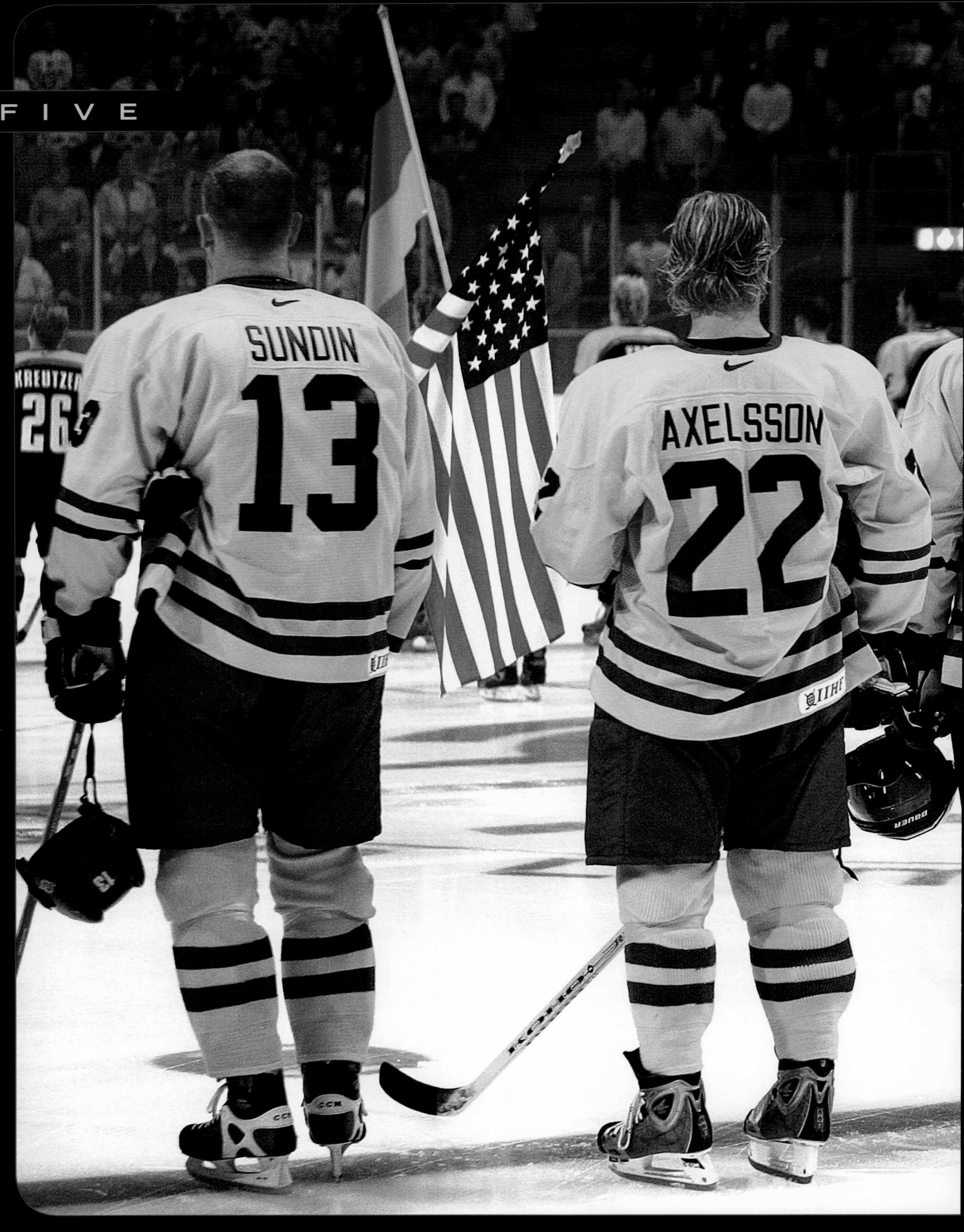
SUNDIN
13
KREUTZER
26
AXELSSON
22
IIHF

It looks so easy for him and I'm a little jealous in that department. Here I am running around and everyone else is running around, but he just seems to find a way to get out of situations and make the easy pass. It was a pleasure to play with him and a pleasure to see him play.

He's as good as they come. He sees the ice and is so mobile and doesn't have to do anything more than he has to. He's all over the ice without even doing anything, it's just so natural. I played with him and of course I remember most of all when he scored the winning goal in the (2006) Olympics. So it's been great knowing him and playing with him. He's a great, great person.

PETER FORSBERG | NHL Center, 1994-2008, 2010-11
Swedish National Team Teammate

Lidstrom appeared several times for his country in world championship and World Cup of Hockey competition, then in 1998, garnered a chance he thought he'd never get when the NHL opted to send its best players to the Winter Olympic Games.

"I think it's real important to players from all ends of the world," Lidstrom said of NHLers playing in the Olympics. "Having a chance to showcase the best players in the world in such a big event, I'm all for having a chance to play in the Olympics for NHL players."

Lidstrom also valued the Olympic Games for the experience, the opportunity to mingle with some of the world's greatest athletes from other winter sports. "I really enjoyed playing in the Olympics," he said. "It wasn't like the World Cup where it was just hockey.

"I liked the Olympic Village with all the other athletes. It was a much bigger stage with all kinds of other things going on."

Lidstrom felt this way even though things didn't go well for the Swedes during his first two Olympiads. At Nagano in 1998, Sweden fell 2-1 to Finland in the quarterfinals. Four years later at Salt Lake City, following an unbeaten round-robin performance, the Swedes were stunned 4-3 by Belarus in the quarterfinals, the winning goal coming on Vladimir Krikunov's 80-foot shot that bounced off the head of Swedish goalie Tommy Salo and into the net.

"I thought we were close to doing something great and we collapsed in the quarterfinals," Lidstrom recalled. "That's something we still think about. We started the tournament so well. We beat Canada in the first game, 5-2, and we played real well. We played real well in the following games, too, right up until the quarterfinals when we were a huge favorite against Belarus and then we didn't play up to par.

(Pictured from left to right) Henrik Lundqvist (Rangers), Henrik Sedin (Canucks), Loui Eriksson (Stars), Lidstrom, Daniel Sedin (Canucks), Oliver Ekman-Larsson (Coyotes) and Erik Karlsson (Senators).

NATIONAL ICON

"Ever since I started watching hockey, Nick has always been the No. 1 guy. He's been very successful throughout his career and he's done a lot of great things for a lot of young Swedes, especially me. He's a great role model and winning the Norris Trophy wasn't something that I expected to do this early in my career.

"Obviously he was very successful in what he did and has a lot of respect throughout the league. I don't think I can do the exact same things that he did; I'm a little bit different but he's certainly someone that I always watched and still look to sometimes."

ERIK KARLSSON
Ottawa Senators Defenseman
Norris Trophy Recipient, 2012

Salutes Nicklas Lidstrom

RAM

PLUS+

Lidstrom is among 25 players who are members of the exclusive Triple Gold Club – winners of the Stanley Cup, Olympic gold medal and IIHF World Championship. He is one of eight Red Wings to be part of the club along with Viacheslav Fetisov, Igor Larionov, Brendan Shanahan, Henrik Zetterberg, Jiri Slegr, Mikael Samuelsson and Niklas Kronwall. Detroit coach Mike Babcock is also a member of the Triple Gold Club.

"We didn't play as well as we knew we could. Losing in the quarterfinals was tough. It was tough for everyone on the team. Still to this day you remember the loss. It was a tough loss because a lot of people in Sweden are passionate about the national team and there was a lot of disappointment from the people in Sweden."

It still bothers Lidstrom that his close friend Salo was vilified in his homeland. "He was a player who took a lot of heat for letting in that goal," Lidstrom said. "People didn't say a whole lot. It was more from reading the newspapers and learning of their disappointment that way.

"I actually stopped reading the papers after that. I saw one headline and I knew there was going to be a lot of disappointment,

so I stopped reading the stories about that tournament."

Finally in Turin, there was redemption for Sweden and Lidstrom. The Swedes won the gold medal, downing archrival Finland 3-2 in the gold-medal game. "Sweden and Finland, that's huge," he said. "It's one of the greatest rivalries in all of sports. It goes way back."

Kimmo Timonen gave the Finns the lead until Lidstrom's Red Wings teammate Henrik Zetterberg tied the score. Another Red Wing, Niklas Kronwall, put Sweden ahead before Ville Peltonen tied it for the Finns.

Ten seconds into the third period, from a faceoff at center ice, Mats Sundin won the draw, and then Peter Forsberg got the puck back to Lidstrom, who wired one of his patented slap shots off the crossbar and in behind Finnish netminder Antero Niittymaki.

The tally was the Swedish version of what

SVERIGE
BREV

Nicklas Lidström

5

2013

VÄSTERÅS.
013-08-02.

D. NILSSON / E. WILSSON

To help promote the 2013 World Championships, the Swedish Posten (postal service) released a postage stamp featuring Nicklas Lidstrom, who was enlisted as an ambassador for the medal rounds that took place in Stockholm.

"

He's been an icon in Sweden for so long, two decades, it's a long time playing in the best league in the world. The things that he accomplished are remarkable. No offense to Forsberg and Sundin, but to win four Stanley Cups and seven Norris Trophies that says it all I think. For me growing up, he wasn't my biggest idol because I was too young, but once he started making it in this league, I mean, who doesn't look up to him? He's an icon and everyone wants to be like him, play like him offensively, defensively, you name it. … Just watching him play was just like a symphony.

"

HENRIK TALLINDER   Buffalo Sabres Defenseman
Swedish National Team Teammate

Paul Henderson's winner in the 1972 Summit Series meant to Canada – it was the shot heard round Sweden.

"That shot is going in the history books," Sundin said.

Certainly, it's still remembered fondly today.

"Yeah, people still talk about it," Lidstrom said. "When I'm out and about in Sweden, a lot of people want to talk about that goal. They remember where they were when they watched the game and when I scored the goal. It's a great feeling to hear those people talk about the goal and remembering what they were doing that afternoon."

Making the moment even more memorable was that three players who combined for the gold-medal tally – Lidstrom, Forsberg and Sundin – were the greatest Swedish players of Lidstrom's generation.

"That tournament was special for all of us because we didn't know if we would play in that big of a tournament together again," Lidstrom said. "It turned out that we didn't play together again because Mats didn't play (four years later) in Vancouver.

"In that (2006) tournament, we got better and better as the tournament went along. We played our best in the deciding games, in the quarterfinals and semis, so going into the finals we felt good about ourselves.

"Playing against Finland, we've had our rivalry against that country for a lot of years and it was a big game for both countries, so to come out on top, to win that final game – after having two disappointing tournaments in the Olympics before that – it was such a relief to win an Olympic gold medal. And to win it with

BACK STORY

Lidstrom's biggest goal lifted a nation

It was like a dozen other goals he had scored in his NHL career, but this one had Herculean power to lift a country in jubilation over its chief rival.

Just 10-seconds into the third period of the gold medal game in the 2006 Torino Olympics, Nicklas Lidstrom ripped a 56-foot slap shot that beat Finnish goalie Antero Nittymaki, snapping a 2-2 tie.

Still, there was more than 19-minutes left before the Swedes could claim the Olympic gold for only the second time in their nation's history. But Sweden's lineup was loaded with NHL veterans, veterans like Lidstrom, Mats Sundin and Peter Forsberg, who had been in the hockey trenches before and knew how to handle big-game pressure.

"We were scrambling those last few minutes because Finland was pressing pretty hard," forward Daniel Alfredsson said. "But we had a good core of veterans. I think Nick is one of those guys whose game suits pressure situations more than most. It seems like he liked those situations and he was confident in those and it rubbed off on other people."

Lidstrom's goal – his second of the tournament – eventually held up as the game-winner, making him an instant hockey patriot in Sweden.

"It was a big tournament for us for many reasons, but one of them was that it was probably going to be the last chance to win with all of those big guys, Sundin, Lidstrom and Forsberg," goalie Henrik Lundqvist said. "For me personally, it was my first year in the NHL and to be on the same team with them was very special. But to win the Olympics, obviously, it meant a lot to the country, and for us players it was an amazing experience."

A day after snatching the gold medal, the Swedish team triumphantly returned to Sweden where more than 100,000 hockey-crazed fans greeted them in downtown Stockholm to celebrate the team's stunning achievement.

Winning the gold also preserved Lidstrom's legacy on the international stage as he joined the Triple Gold Club, an elite class of players who have won a Stanley Cup, and gold medals at the Olympics and World Championships.

"Nick's won everything there is to win, and topping that off with an Olympic gold is pretty special," Alfredsson said. "But what really made it special was getting the reception back in Sweden and seeing how much it really means to all Swedes. Getting all of that appreciation was really special."

The Torino Games also represented the first international gold medal for Alfredsson, who would play with Lidstrom on seven different Swedish national teams, the first time at the 1996 World Cup of Hockey.

"I didn't know much about him, to be honest," Alfredsson said. "I had one season in the NHL and had played twice against him. I guessed he was a pretty good player, but didn't know too much about him."

Over the years, Alfredsson, albeit a forward, learned plenty from Lidstrom.

"Early in your career you watch and pick up on stuff all of the time," Alfredsson said. "Obviously with Nick – having been so successful in the NHL as well, winning four Cups and being around as long as he has been and around so many great players – there's lots to learn.

"But the biggest thing I found was how he was able to push himself as much as he did, day in and day out, to be better all of the time, even though he had been so good. That's a talent in itself and something I admired."

the guys that I played a lot of tournaments with, including Forsberg and Sundin, and to have those two assist on the goal that I scored to be the deciding goal was the best. I thought it was a perfect ending that they assisted on my goal.

"I'd rank it right up there with winning the Stanley Cup. The Stanley Cup is played every year. The Olympics are played every fourth year. That's what makes it so tough to win. I'm just glad we finally did it. Finally being able to wear the gold medal was just an unbelievable feeling."

The 2006 Olympic win, coupled with his 1991 world title and his four Stanley Cup championships captured as a Red Wing put Lidstrom among a very exclusive group. He's one of 25 players who have gained membership in the Triple Gold Club.

"That's very special too," Lidstrom said. "Not a whole lot of players have been able to do that, win two different tournaments with the national team then winning the Stanley Cup as well. It's a special feeling and something that I'm very proud of, to be a part of that Triple Gold Club."

In 2010, Lidstrom completed his national team career by captaining the Swedish team to a quarterfinal appearance at the Vancouver Olympic Games. His fellow Swedes think his many achievements make Lidstrom unique and legendary in Swedish hockey circles. "The things he has accomplished are remarkable," Buffalo Sabres defenseman Henrik Tallinder said. "In my eyes, he's the best Swedish player we've had over here."

When you factor in all of his accomplishments on the ice, combined with his comportment away from the rink, many of Lidstrom's countrymen view him as the model of what a Swedish hockey player should strive to be.

"He has been a great role model for every Swede growing up, myself included," New Jersey Devils goalie Johan Hedberg said. "He's a great person and very, very professional. I think he's someone who probably doesn't get the respect he deserves in Sweden. He's a low-key guy who gets overshadowed by some more marquee personalities.

"If there's anyone who people should want to model themselves after, it would be him." **5**

"

I met him for the first, and only time at the 2009 Stanley Cup finals the year that I was drafted. He was one of those guys that you really looked up to, and obviously, Detroit always had a lot of Swedes on the team, so they were a team that I followed a lot. Meeting him was special, very special. It was a very busy schedule, but when I got to meet him and speak some Swedish with him it was a lot of fun.

Just seeing him play, it was unreal, the way he plays, the way he moves on the blue line and the way he gets pucks to the net, he's a very special player. It's one thing to idolize him, but to try and emulate him isn't an easy thing to do. He always made those hard plays look simple and that's how you need a defenseman to play, just simple in your own end.

"

VICTOR HEDMAN | Tampa Bay Lightning Defenseman

5 FIVE

The Consummate Leader

Lidstrom's ascension to Detroit's captaincy made history in Hockeytown and Sweden

As the Red Wings took the ice for their 2006-07 season opener at Joe Louis Arena against the Vancouver Canucks, a major announcement was about to be made, but it would simply reveal the worst-kept secret in Hockeytown – that Nicklas Lidstrom was to succeed the retired Steve Yzerman as captain of the team.

Lidstrom received a minute-long standing ovation from the Wings' faithful, along with a formal passing of the torch from the former captain, Yzerman, who conducted the ceremonial opening faceoff between Lidstrom and another Swedish captain, Vancouver's Markus Naslund.

Lidstrom would follow the likes of Naslund, Toronto's Mats Sundin and Ottawa's Daniel Alfredsson in becoming yet another Swedish captain in the NHL, although his Red Wing teammate and fellow Swedish defenseman Andreas Lilja felt Lidstrom being picked captain had more to do with character than nationality.

"
There was so much said about him. How good he is, what great hands he has, how well he can see the ice. Everything is great about him, but what is most important, as a goalie, is you can depend on him every night. He never takes the night off. He's always ready in every situation. Very, very rarely he made mistakes.
"

DOMINIK HASEK | NHL Goalie, 1990-2008
Red Wings Teammate, 2001-04, 2006-08

·1997 STANLEY CUP CHAMPIONS·

inside
HOCKEYTOWN
THE OFFICIAL PUBLICATION OF THE DETROIT RED WINGS
NOVEMBER 1997
$5.00

A BANNER NIGHT

Darren McCarty fights for life
• Masked Men: Chris Osgood & Kevin Hodson • Stats, trivia & much more! • Larry Murphy takes stock with the Wings

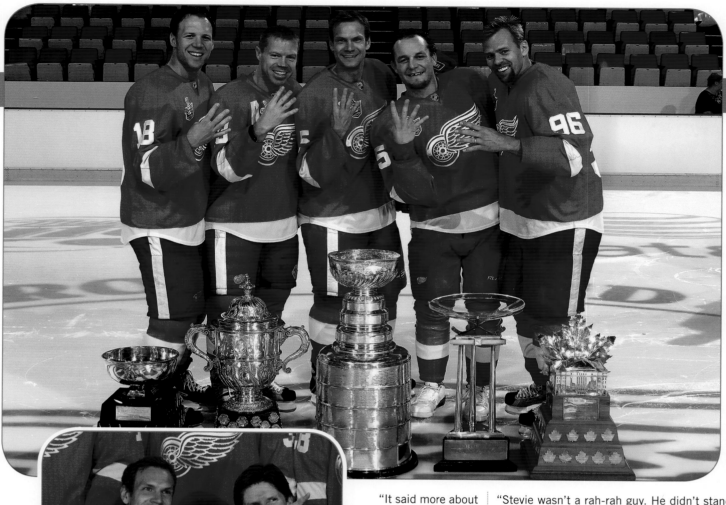

"It said more about the guys they pick to be captain than it did for Swedish hockey," Lilja said. "He (Lidstrom) was an unbelievable leader. He's down to earth. He didn't say much, but he said something when he needed to.

"He always put himself out there. He never had dips in his game. You'd never see Nicklas play a bad game. Same thing with Steve, he never had a bad game, he gave everything he had."

Those who'd played under Yzerman's legendary leadership saw similar qualities in Lidstrom's style and game.

"He's a quiet guy, he's a lot like Steve," former Detroit forward Kirk Maltby said.

"Stevie wasn't a rah-rah guy. He didn't stand up between periods and kind of blast somebody, or the team. He said things to individuals or the team when it needed to be said, whether it was in the playoffs or in the regular season during a losing streak.

"He (Yzerman) led by example and Nick did the same thing. He said things when he needed to and everyone knew he'd lead by example on the ice."

Lidstrom's consistent play between the boards was perhaps his best quality as a leader. "You'd be hard-pressed to find a bad stretch where Nick was not Nick," Maltby said. "It's unheard of. Right up until his last game in the league, he was considered for the Norris Trophy."

Coming off a 2005-06 season in which he posted career-highs in assists (64) and points (80), there was no questioning that Lidstrom was at the top of his game and in the prime of his career at both ends of the rink.

HULL OF A MAN

When it came to Nicklas Lidstrom, both members of a Hockey Hall of Fame family viewed him as a Hull of a player.

"If I had to pick any player to start building my team, Lidstrom would be the guy," Chicago Blackhawks legend Bobby Hull said.

Bobby's son Brett Hull, Lidstrom's teammate on Detroit's 2001-02 Stanley Cup-winning club, couldn't agree more. "I never played with or against a better defenseman and I played with some outstanding defensemen," Brett Hull said.

Thanks for the memories **meijer**®

PLUS

When Lidstrom played his 1,000th NHL game Feb. 29, 2004 against the Philadelphia Flyers, he'd appeared in 1,000 of a possible 1,017 regular-season games during his career to that point. "I don't know that there's been a player that's gotten to 1,000 games faster," then-Detroit coach Dave Lewis said.

"He didn't get enough credit for his defense," Yzerman said. "He was one of the top defensive defensemen in the league, but you can't say that enough about him. His play was always really strong.

"Lidstrom's the best player I played with."

While Yzerman was certainly the face of Detroit's three Stanley Cup winners, Lidstrom was the backbone. His stalwart, almost mistake-free defensive play was the envy of opposition coaches, who all dreamed of finding a Lidstrom to anchor their blue-line.

"A classy individual," Nashville Predators coach Barry Trotz said. "When you talk about people who exude what a hockey player should be, people like Nick and Yzerman come to the forefront.

"They really have a lot of respect for the game and its history."

A respect that was mutual amongst Lidstrom's peers. Mark Messier, who remains the only man to captain two different teams to the Stanley Cup – the Edmonton Oilers in 1990 and the New York Rangers in 1994 – saw greatness in Lidstrom's style of leadership.

"He was the prototypical leader by example," Messier said. "If you talk about a consistent leader, he was the same guy game in and game out, he was consistent in his personality so that when the guys looked at him, he was always going to be the same guy.

"He had some tough shoes to fill with Yzerman leaving there, and he stepped in and they didn't miss a beat."

Former Detroit center Kris Draper won four Stanley Cups with the Wings – three with Yzerman as captain and the latter with Lidstrom in charge and saw similarities in the way they led both on and off the ice.

"First of all, Nick was a tremendous captain," Draper said. "When Stevie decided to retire, it was a no-brainer who was going to be the next captain of this hockey club. And Nick was very similar to Stevie in how he carried himself on and off the ice. Really, what he did is he'd just go out and lead by example, playing at a high level, game in, game out.

"As captain, Nick became a little bit more vocal. As a leader of the team, obviously he felt there were sometimes, some situations where he had to say something. He didn't say a lot. He was not a rah-rah kind of guy. But

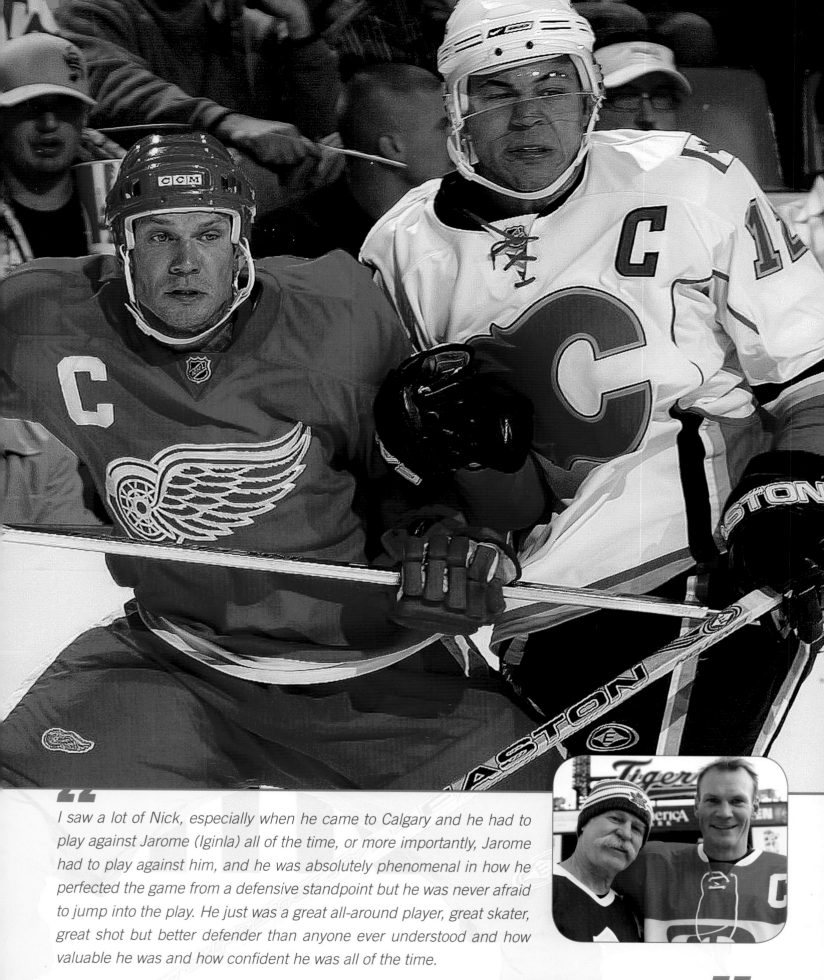

"

I saw a lot of Nick, especially when he came to Calgary and he had to play against Jarome (Iginla) all of the time, or more importantly, Jarome had to play against him, and he was absolutely phenomenal in how he perfected the game from a defensive standpoint but he was never afraid to jump into the play. He just was a great all-around player, great skater, great shot but better defender than anyone ever understood and how valuable he was and how confident he was all of the time.

"

LANNY McDONALD | NHL Right Wing, 1973-89
1992 HOF Inductee

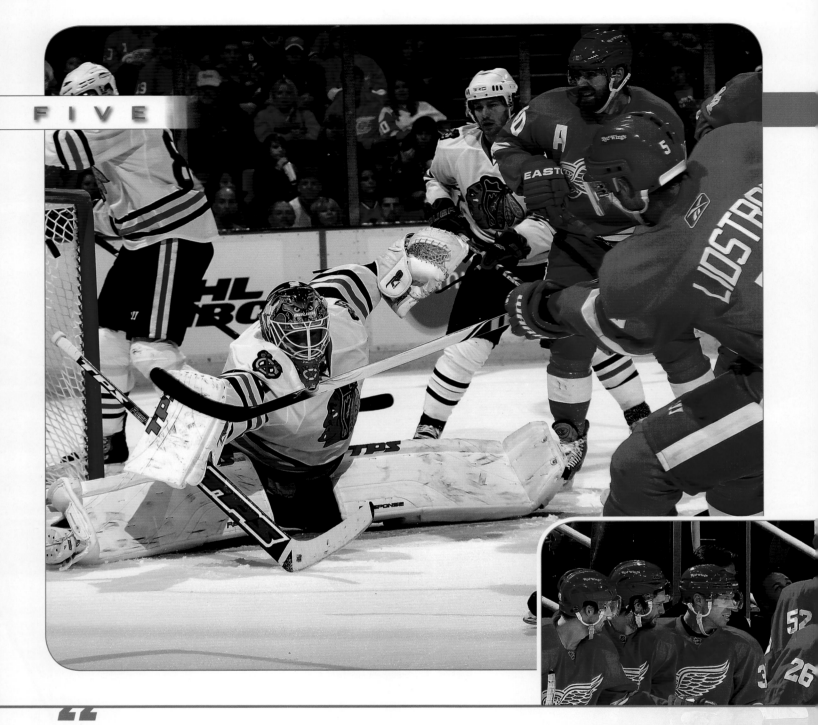

"

I think as a defenseman, we all look up to him and what he was able to do in his career and the way he played the game and carried himself off the ice. I know we all kind of watched him, even playing against him, trying to learn as much as we could. I think his statistics and resume speak for themselves. Seven Norris Trophies and everything he was able to accomplish in Detroit, being the captain, the first European captain and to win a Stanley Cup, it just goes on and on.

Obviously he was doing something right. I'm proud to have my name on the same trophy as him. That says it all. He was able to control the game with the way he thought the game, just his Hockey IQ and positioning ... his ability to defend and his ability to create offense. Just all-around, he's a true defenseman. He wasn't just offensive. He played the game the right way and got his points the right way, not by running around trying to be a forward.

"

DUNCAN KEITH   Chicago Blackhawks Defenseman
Norris Trophy Recipient, 2010

just like Stevie and a lot of the great leaders, when they spoke, everyone listened."

Lidstrom believed he learned a lot from Yzerman in a decade-long apprenticeship — about preparation, about how you carry yourself, things like that. But he also acknowledged some changes, however slight, in his approach to the job.

"I think I was more vocal, especially in the room, maybe than I was in the past as assistant captain," Lidstrom said. "I tried to talk to some of the younger players a little bit more, encourage them and try to help them out a little bit. The same thing on the back end, too, with my defensive partners. You wanted to be a little bit more vocal and try and help them out."

There was little that Lidstrom didn't bring to the table, with or without a 'C' sewn to his Red Wings jersey.

"We're very lucky to be playing with one of the greatest," Draper said. "Not only the

greatest defenseman of all time, but one of the greatest players that this game has seen."

With four Norris Trophies wins in the previous five seasons, there was no questioning Lidstrom's ability. And as for his personality, it was even more first-class than his work between the boards.

"There is absolutely nothing negative about him," said teammate and close friend Tomas Holmstrom. "He skated so well, he was able to cut players off all the time. He played 30 minutes a game. He scored. He made other guys better; he was great on the power play. He scored shorthanded goals."

Lidstrom carried the team by making others around him better players, the true mark of greatness.

"What's not to like about him?" asked fellow Detroit defenseman Niklas Kronwall. "He was by far the best defenseman in the world. He made it look so easy. I don't know if he ever got tired out there."

the BACK STORY

Lidstrom's leadership, friendship went beyond the rink

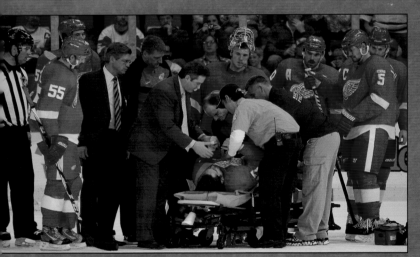

Patrick Eaves was in a vastly dark place, both literally and figuratively.

For months after a speeding puck crashed into the side of his head, the Red Wings' fourth-line winger battled concussion-like symptoms that brought on nausea and intolerable headaches for days on end. Spending hours alone in a quiet, dark room provided only the slightest glimmer of tranquility.

Even after his surgically repaired jaw healed he continued to suffer through the indescribable neurological damage done to his brain. "I couldn't be a parent, I couldn't be a father. I couldn't be a husband," Eaves said. "For about six to eight weeks my head hurt so bad that I couldn't sleep."

Katie Eaves was four-months pregnant with the couple's second daughter when the injury occurred in November 2011. She's a nurse, and that helped matters at home, but what wasn't expected was the compassion and thoughtfulness shown by the Red Wings' team captain. Every day Nicklas Lidstrom visited Eaves' Northville home just to check

on his teammate and to bring him his favorite chocolate shake.

"I don't even know how he knew I liked those shakes," Eaves said. "But that was the biggest thing, that he cared enough to do that. That goes a long way, but that's who he is. It wasn't like he thought, 'Well, if I act this way I'll be looked at as a leader.' That's what makes him a great person and made him a great leader."

Eaves arrived in Detroit in time for the fourth season of Lidstrom's captaincy. It was the summer of 2009 when Eaves signed a free agent deal and moved into a suburban neighborhood where he quickly befriended Lidstrom and Tomas Holmstrom, who lived in the area. The three regularly carpooled to Joe Louis Arena on game days.

"I didn't know anything about him off of the ice. Just played against him once and he was way better than everyone," Eaves said of

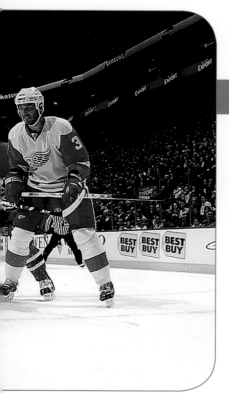

Another element of Lidstrom's game that impressed Detroit coach Mike Babcock was that when the NHL cracked down on obstruction following the 2004-05 lockout, while many defensemen struggled to adjust to a game where they couldn't utilize their stick and body to impede opponents, Lidstrom didn't miss a beat.

"There was no player, in my opinion, on the back end in the NHL that was like this guy," Babcock said. "He was the best in the last (style of) game and he was the best in this (style of) game. It seems to me he was the best in any game."

Lidstrom admitted that the transition to the new NHL was probably easier for him than any other defenseman in the league. "I always tried to play with my positioning," he said. "I think it was more important than ever when the rule changes came in. You couldn't use your stick as much, so you had to play your position better.

Lidstrom. "But right away, as the new person who walks into the room he made me feel like I was one of the guys from day one.

"We just seemed to hit it off and just had a really cool friendship. It was nice to be welcomed in like that, especially by the captain."

The teammates became really close friends, occasionally going to lunch or stopping for coffee at Starbucks. Eaves grew to admire Lidstrom as more than a hockey player and teammate. So it wasn't unusual for Eaves to seek advice on non-hockey topics, particularly parenting tips, from Lidstrom, whose sons are much older than the Eaves girls.

"He's a really good family man, so I looked up to him in that sense," Eaves said. "Once we started having little ones of our own he was always there to bounce questions off of when it came to being a good dad and being a part of things. That was always nice to have, somebody who has been through it

already with the little kids."

But words couldn't describe the outpouring of sympathy Lidstrom felt when he saw his friend crumple to the ice, then wheeled away on a stretcher to a waiting ambulance inside Joe Louis Arena. The sound alone of vulcanized rubber crashing into Eaves' skull was all Lidstrom needed to know his friend was in trouble.

"When he took that shot to the head I was on the ice standing almost right behind him, but close to the net," recalled Lidstrom. "I was one of the first players to come up to him on the ice. He was in a lot of pain and I felt terrible for him."

It was then that the captain made a commitment to Eaves, but kept it to himself.

"When you see someone go down like that, he's your teammate, you're battling with him every night," Lidstrom said. "To know that he was in so much pain I wanted to go by his house and make sure that he was OK, or if I could do anything for him when I went down

to The Joe every day. I wanted to make sure he was OK, because it was scary."

Eaves spent a few days in the hospital, where his jaws were wired shut. His teammates all visited, but Lidstrom tracked his friend's recovery beyond his discharge from the Detroit Medical Center.

"I was pretty out of it, in a bad place," Eaves said. "But he did come visit and was always checking in on me, whether stopping by or via text."

Nov. 26, 2011 was the last time Eaves and Lidstrom were on the ice together as teammates, but they'll always remain friends.

"I miss him," Eaves said. "Homer and Nick are gone now and they're my friends. I don't see them as much now. I see Nick when he comes into town and we go grab lunch. I didn't look at Nick as the legend that he is, like Homer, he's just my friend. They're good people, who I liked to hang around with and we had a lot of good laughs."

"That's pretty much what I did my whole career."

When asked what made Lidstrom arguably the premier defenseman of his generation, Babcock is at a loss to define specifics.

"He was just flat out good and he didn't know why either," Babcock said. "He just had that ability. I don't know why he could make the right pass all the time, the right play all the time and hold up the check and shoot the puck. But, I can tell you it had nothing to with coaching.

"I've never coached anybody this good, never coached anybody as consistent, as intuitive, who has a great understanding of the game and is tuned into what's going on. Nick Lidstrom, in my opinion, was as good a

leader as you can have in sports. His presence, his ability, how calm he was and how driven he was. He was as competitive as they come and he won everything. Never mind his skill, in my mind, his steadying force was instrumental.

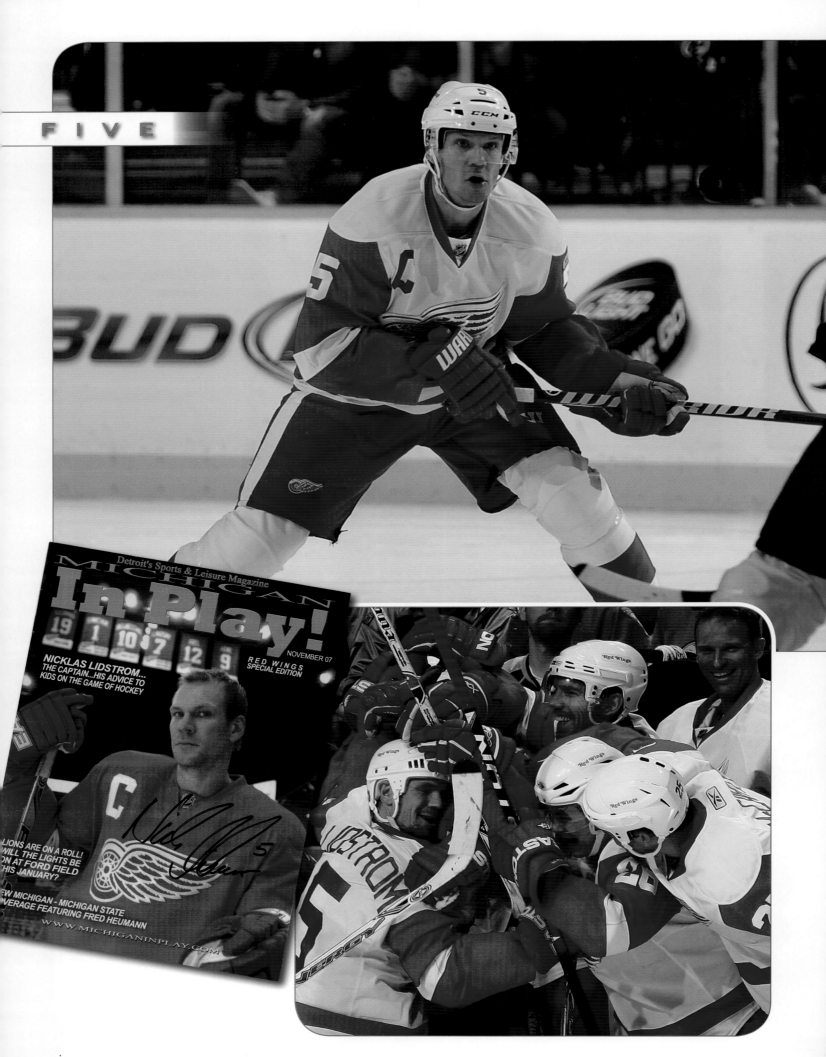

Detroit's Sports & Leisure Magazine

MICHIGAN In Play!

NOVEMBER 07

19 **1** **10** **7** **12** **9**

RED WINGS
SPECIAL EDITION

NICKLAS LIDSTROM...
THE CAPTAIN...HIS ADVICE TO
KIDS ON THE GAME OF HOCKEY

LIONS ARE ON A ROLL!
WILL THE LIGHTS BE
ON AT FORD FIELD
THIS JANUARY?

EW MICHIGAN - MICHIGAN STATE
VERAGE FEATURING FRED HEUMANN

WWW.MICHIGANINPLAY.COM

"He's just a special person. The most humble superstar I've ever met."

A humble man, whose subtle genius made him the best player on the ice, night after night.

"He was the biggest constant for the Red Wings for years," former Detroit goalie Chris Osgood said. "He was great from the first time he played here. I know he got his rewards but he wasn't talked about enough.

"When people asked about our team, he was always the fifth or sixth guy mentioned. They'd mention (Pavel) Datsyuk, (Henrik) Zetterberg, Dom (Hasek), some other guys and then Lidstrom on defense. It was always, 'And then Lidstrom on defense.'

"But really, he was our guy. I'm sure teams said, 'We have to neutralize Lidstrom,' but very rarely did that happen."

The reason for that, according to Detroit general manager Ken Holland, was simple to explain.

"Nick was the best defenseman in the world for several years," Holland said. "He was a great captain and role model who did everything right both on and off the ice.

"With Nick, we felt we were one of the elite teams in the NHL and a Stanley Cup contender. If we didn't have him — a defenseman who plays 30 minutes against the other team's best players and still scores – we'd have fallen quite a bit because he had that big of an impact.

"He wowed you because he never had a bad game and never made a mistake night after night after night, year after year after year. That's how I got wowed."

Carrying the team on his shoulders, via both his presence and his performance, Lidstrom lifted his teammates up to his high standard.

"You'd see the way Nick played at such a high level," Draper said. "You wanted to be there right with him. It was just great to be playing with such a great leader, such a great captain." **5**

5 FIVE

Generational Star

Hockey people view Lidstrom as the greatest player of his era

FIVE

In the midst of the 1998 Stanley Cup finals between the defending champion Detroit Red Wings and the Washington Capitals, the NHL gathered its top prospects in that spring's entry draft for a media opportunity.

Among the group on display was Regina Pats defenseman Brad Stuart, and as excited as he was to briefly be the center of attention on hockey's biggest stage, it paled in comparison to the fact that he got to meet Red Wings defenseman Nicklas Lidstrom at the morning skate that day.

"He's my favorite player," Stuart said at the time. "I just love the way he plays. I think he's the best defenseman in the NHL."

A decade later, as the Wings pursued another Stanley Cup title, they opted to bolster their defense for the stretch run, acquiring Stuart from the Los Angeles Kings.

Suddenly, Stuart was the teammate of his hero and getting to see Lidstrom up close and personal on a nightly basis only left Stuart more in awe of Lidstrom's greatness. In 2010-11, as Lidstrom won his seventh Norris Trophy, he frequently skated in a pairing with Stuart.

"He played one of the best seasons I've ever seen a defenseman play," Stuart said. "For anybody to have a season like that is pretty incredible, and then you factor in he'd been playing for 20 years, and it's even that much more amazing."

Amazing and Lidstrom were frequently combined in sentences when hockey people attempted to explain away what it was that put Lidstrom a notch above all other defensemen of his era.

"He was just consistently the workhorse on our team, kind of the backbone of the whole team," former Detroit captain Steve Yzerman said.

PLUS

In 2011, Lidstrom became the oldest player in NHL history, at 41 years and 57 days, to win the Norris Trophy.

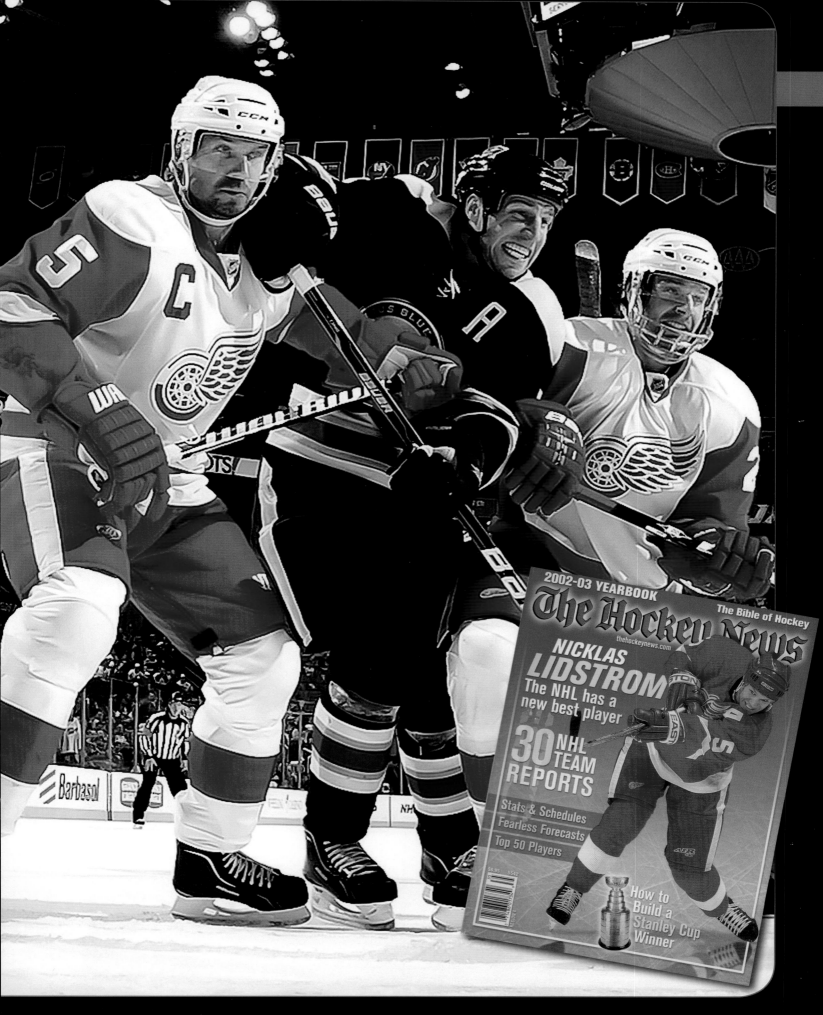

2002-03 YEARBOOK

The Hockey News

The Bible of Hockey

thehockeynews.com

NICKLAS LIDSTROM
The NHL has a new best player

30 NHL TEAM REPORTS

Stats & Schedules
Fearless Forecasts
Top 50 Players

How to Build a Stanley Cup Winner

$8.95

THE BENCHMARK

"*Where do I start? He's one of those guys that we still talk about. When Detroit went on the power play and Lidstrom had the puck at the point you're kind of thinking – and you don't want to admit it – but you're kind of thinking it's usually going to end up in the back of the net. He was so good and so calm, some of the things that he did you've rarely ever seen in the history of the game. He just had a style that no one could ever really emulate I guess. He was an amazing player.*

"*Usually he was getting the better of me. He was always in such good position. He was never overexerting himself, he was always calm and he knew how to handle every single situation like he just drew up the math equation in his head beforehand. He was just tough to predict when he had the puck and even tougher to keep it away from because he was such a smart defender.*"

JONATHAN TOEWS
Chicago Blackhawks Captain
Conn Smythe Trophy Recipient, 2010

Salutes Nicklas Lidstrom

"

He's probably one of the greatest players I've played against. He was unbelievable. His skills and his skating ability and puck control were tremendous. You don't want to make mistakes when he's on the ice because it can cost you a lot, it can cost you a goal or a big turnover. He can play almost 60 minutes out there and still be the best. He didn't make lots of moves; he knows exactly where he had to be position-wise. Of course, he wasn't injured much, so that's huge, but most of the time it's all about, you know, exactly what to do at that time.

"

ALEXANDER OVECHKIN | Washington Capitals Captain

"Nick drove the bus here," Wings coach Mike Babcock added. "In my mind, his steadying force was instrumental. Never mind his skill level – just who he is as a man.

"Lidstrom, I think just with his everyday professionalism and the modeling he did for the rest of us and how he carried himself, how he handled himself, how well he played, how hard he practiced, how good of a fitness level he maintained, was an example to everybody.

"Obviously he was a gifted, gifted athlete who read the game as good as anybody and played in all situations. So he was real important for us, and when your best defensive defenseman is your best offensive defenseman, I think it helps, because you get the puck going.

"To appreciate the subtleties of how talented and consistent he is, you had to watch him every day. He was not about flashy."

Lidstrom beat teams with his intelligence and instincts, a wicked combination that always seemed to put him in the right place to make a play or prevent one.

"He was smart," Wayne Gretzky said. "He might have been the smartest defenseman in the game. He didn't ever have to

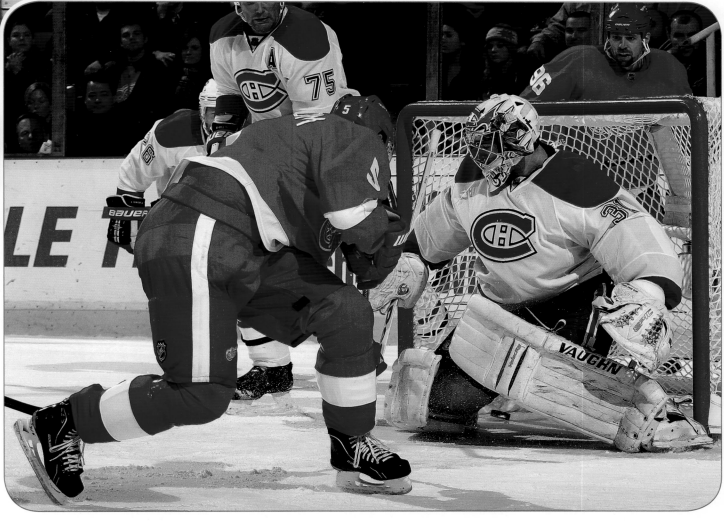

FIVE

overcompensate. He was always in the right position. His angles were as good or better than anyone who ever played the game."

Lidstrom was never as dynamic as Bobby Orr. He wasn't as punishing as Scott Stevens. And that's why his brilliance was often understated.

"He was not the fastest. He didn't have an overpowering shot. He was not the most physical," explained former NHL center Bill Clement, today an NHL television analyst. "But he was a composite of everything you need to be an incredible player. His hockey IQ was off the charts. His anticipation of what was happening on the ice was flawless. His execution was almost always without a mistake.

"When you put all of the components together, I consider him the greatest defensive defenseman of all time."

Even those who played alongside him sheepishly admit that they sometimes overlooked Lidstrom's consistent excellence.

"I didn't realize how good he was until I started playing with him and I'm a Swede. I should know," said Henrik Zetterberg, who succeeded Lidstrom as Detroit's captain. "To me, he was the best, night in and night out for us. It was just awesome to be able to play with him."

Former Red Wing Mickey Redmond, who saw Lidstrom's entire career from the broadcast booth as an analyst on Detroit telecasts, felt there's a reason casual fans usually didn't assess Lidstrom among the all-time great defenders.

"Nick doesn't get the credit or recognition he deserves because he played the game without being physical," Redmond said. "Doug Harvey was a lot like that. When you have a marvelous mind, you can keep yourself out of trouble and avoid getting hurt."

Scotty Bowman, Lidstrom's coach for nine seasons, including a trio of Stanley Cup wins, also coached Harvey with the St. Louis Blues and can compare the two men who each garnered seven Norris Trophy wins.

"They controlled the game," Bowman said. "They both had the same concept. The resulting play they made was not to give the puck away. They made plays. They had the ability to control the game, mainly because of their ability to pass the puck at the right time and play the point.

"When I look at a defenseman, when he gets the puck, what is the resulting play? Does his team keep the puck or does the other team get it? Over 95 percent of the time, when Lidstrom had the puck, one of his teammates got it.

"I was always amazed. I don't remember him getting caught up the ice and leaving his defense partner to defend an out-numbered situation. It was just uncanny the way his whole game evolved. He was so good at keeping the puck.

Lidstrom is a legend in this game. To get a chance to play with him and be on the same team and see how professional he is just something that I'll definitely not forget. You see how calm, cool and collected he is, and on the ice you see how patient he is with the puck. It's amazing when you see those types of things when you see it on the highlights, but until you see it first-hand you don't appreciate it as much. I'm sure the guys on Detroit's team appreciated it a lot too. He's so professional and that's what this game is all about.

STEVEN STAMKOS | Tampa Bay Lightning Center
Played on Team Lidstrom in 2011 All-Star G

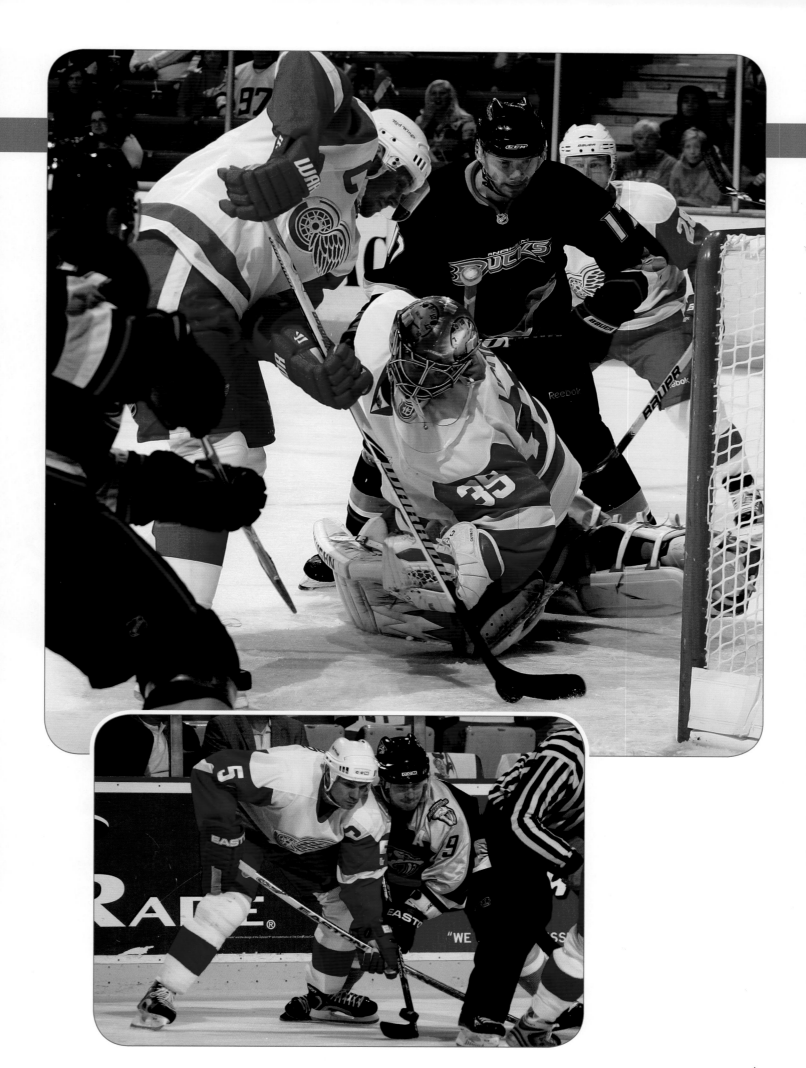

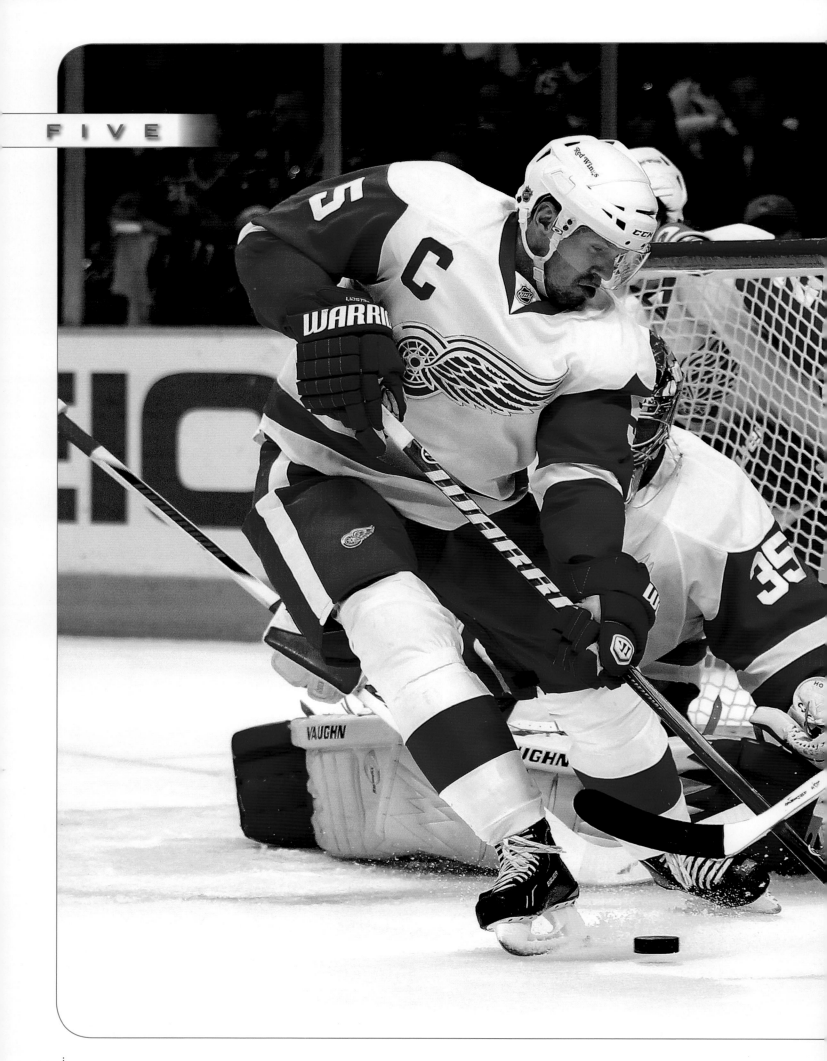

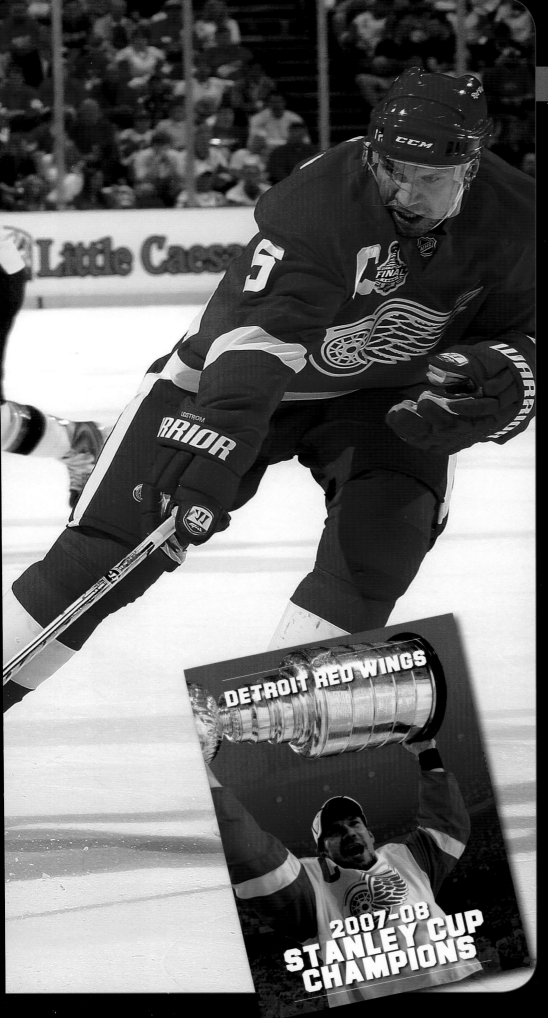

DETROIT RED WINGS

2007-08 STANLEY CUP CHAMPIONS

"He made my life pretty easy, I'll tell you that. He was just a wonderful player. One of a kind. As to who's the best ever . . . it's tough to rate this guy here and that guy there. I will say I don't rate anyone ahead of Lidstrom, though."

You'd have a hard time finding anyone who played with him that would disagree with Bowman's assessment.

"I don't think people realize, still, how good he really was," Detroit and Swedish teammate Niklas Kronwall said of Lidstrom. "There's no one like him, and there probably never will be another guy like him."

Those who had to face Lidstrom were equally impressed by his never-ending dominance, even if it wasn't often front-page news.

"What can you say about a guy who is probably one of the best defensemen to ever play hockey?" Dallas Stars defenseman Sergei Gonchar said. "He controlled the puck on the power play. He was great defensively. He's always pretty much in a perfect position. He played a lot of minutes for them. He does everything."

Or, as Hall of Famer and former Norris Trophy winner Al MacInnis put it: "Has there been a smarter player, ever, than Nick Lidstrom?"

With his combination of hockey smarts, economy of movement and seemingly extra-sensory anticipatory skills, Lidstrom was a constant source of frustration to those seeking to gain any advantage against the Red Wings.

"He had all the tools," Pittsburgh

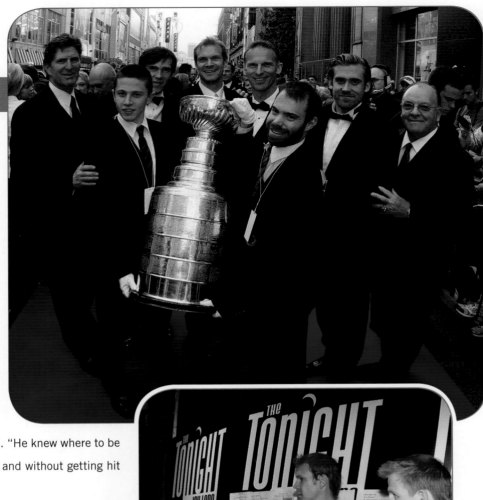

Penguins captain Sidney Crosby said. "He was a big guy; he was smart, read the play well, used his stick to poke check, get in the way and create havoc that way, too. On top of that, he moved the puck and got himself out of trouble a lot. He was a complete package."

Added Crosby's teammate defenseman Kris Letang: "He was a great example for every defenseman in the league. He was amazing."

There's that word again.

"Nick's intelligence is what set him apart," former Dallas forward Mike Modano said. "He knew where to be all the time without having to overexert himself and without getting hit too often.

"It was frustrating playing against him. He wasn't physically wearing you down, but he was always in the way with his body or his stick and you just couldn't get away from him."

Boston Bruins forward Jarome Iginla felt that frustration in two head-to-head playoff matchups against Lidstrom when he was with the Calgary Flames.

"He was a tough guy to play against," Iginla said. "It wasn't physically extremely tough, but he was so smart, quick and he had such a good stick."

Nashville Predators general manager David Poile twice watched the Lidstrom-led Wings bounce his club from the playoffs and tipped his cap in admiration. "I think he's the most efficient player at any position in the history of our game," Poile said.

Detroit goaltender Jimmy Howard got to see that pained look in many an opposing attacker's eyes when all that stood between them and his net was the imposing figure of Lidstrom.

"When you'd watch a guy come down the ice and see No. 5 in front, you could see the look of frustration come over their face," Howard said. "They usually just dumped it in."

Lidstrom made manning the most demanding position on the ice look easy. "He's one of the easiest players I've coached for sure," Babcock said. "You just put him on the ice and got out of the way.

Babcock summed up Lidstrom's place and stature within the game succinctly. "He was a phenomenal player, he was a generational-type player," Babcock said. "Everyone's going to know who he was long after he's done playing." **5**

Pairing with an Ace

When it came to the Stanley Cup finals, Lidstrom had been there and done that – with several partners.

He was the Elizabeth Taylor of the Stanley Cup, frequently changing significant others while continuing to collect the baubles of success. In five Stanley Cup finals appearances, he skated alongside four different defense partners.

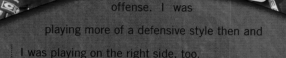

For starters, there was Paul Coffey in Detroit's 1995 loss to New Jersey. Larry Murphy climbed aboard for 1997 (Philadelphia) and 1998 (Washington) wins and Fredrik Olausson worked in tandem with Lidstrom for the 2002 Cup triumph over Carolina. Brian Rafalski was Lidstrom's partner in his last Cup triumph over Pittsburgh in 2008.

Lidstrom believes Rafalski was his best all-around partner – and that's saying something, considering Coffey and Murphy are honored members of the Hockey Hall of Fame.

"I think Rafi was probably the best skater," Lidstrom said. "He covered a lot of ice with his speed. He was the most skilled guy I've played with at both ends, offensively and defensively.

"He made quick passes and quick decisions. Then, there was his smartness with the puck. He was always making the right plays."

Over the span of his career, a trend was constant among Lidstrom's partners. They generally enjoyed career years skating alongside the perennial Norris Trophy winner.

"That wasn't by accident," Wings coach Mike Babcock said. "He (Lidstrom) was just that good. He made the people around him better."

That was the case with Lidstrom's partners in 2005-06 (Andreas Lilja) and 2006-07 (Danny Markov) and in 2007-08 Rafalski netted a career-high 13 goals and equaled his career best of 55 points.

"It didn't matter who we put him with," recalled former Detroit forward Kirk Maltby.

Lidstrom insists playing alongside each of his previous mates proved to be beneficial for him as well.

"Coffey, he was such a great skater," Lidstrom said. "You'd go D to D with him and he could carry it up through the neutral zone. With his great speed, he was good at jumping up and becoming part of the offense. I was playing more of a defensive style then and I was playing on the right side, too.

"Murph was very smart with the puck. He knew when to get rid of it, when to hang on and make plays. He was great at hanging on at the blue-line and keeping pucks in.

"I think our styles were pretty similar and that's why we play so well together. I think it clicked right away when we were put together. It was easy to play with Murph. He was always there for a pass and to help you out. He was always an out for me and Freddy was the same way."

Lidstrom's partners bow in reverence to the greatness they shared the ice with on game night.

"You could tell right away that he was special," Coffey said. "I know people are always saying that after the fact, but this was so obvious. The one word that best described Nick Lidstrom when he and I played as a pair is the same word that best describes him now – poise.

"He was smart. And smart never goes out of style."

In the spring of 1997, Detroit coach Scotty Bowman deployed the guile of Lidstrom and Murphy to completely flummox Philadelphia's physically imposing Legion of Doom line of Eric Lindros, Mikael Renberg and John LeClair.

"Murphy and Lidstrom made a joke out of that forward line," remembered Hall of Fame defenseman Denis Potvin. "They were three steps ahead of them, four games in a row."

Murphy gives much of the credit for their success to Lidstrom. "He made your game a lot easier," he said. "He liked to play the control game and liked to make the play with the puck.

"I'd say he was the best partner I had in my career."

Several other defensemen who were fortunate enough to play alongside Lidstrom would say the same thing.

5 FIVE

The Perfect Human

The Lidstrom way was the right way, plain and simple

I n 2008, Sports Illustrated penned a feature on Nicklas Lidstrom, touting him as a Hart Trophy contender. The article was titled "Mr. Perfect," an apt descriptive of what Lidstrom brought to the ice.

"He was about as perfect of a hockey player as anyone could be," fellow Swedish defenseman Douglas Murray said.

Coaches, teammates, opponents, oldtimers, even those who worked behind the scenes, share the same opinion. It's how they came up with Lidstrom's nickname – The Perfect Human.

"It's really a wonderful tribute to him," former Detroit coach Scotty Bowman said. "You look at what Nicklas Lidstrom did and he was just about a perfect player on the ice."

Lidstrom's style and demeanor reminded Bowman of former Montreal Canadiens great Serge Savard, another legendary defenseman who like Lidstrom won the Conn Smythe Trophy, but whose steady, reliable game was often overshadowed by the other stars in the Habs' lineup.

"He didn't get the attention of the other guys in Montreal, but I saw him play almost a near-perfect game," Bowman said. "Guys like Serge and Lidstrom didn't make mistakes, they played at their own pace."

Opponents sought to punish Lidstrom, but they couldn't hurt him.

"You wanted to put this guy through the boards every time he touched the puck, but he'd find a way to slither around you," former NHL forward Jeff O'Neill explained. "You'd never see him get crushed because he was so smart positionally. It's not like he bailed out or anything. He always maneuvered himself in the right way.

"In my opinion, he was the league's best defenseman."

Attempting to rattle him or trying to throw him off his game with psychological warfare was pointless. "He was a frustrating guy to

Nick's exceptional, just a class act, I mean, the guy is a Hall of Famer, arguably the best of all time. Nick Lidstrom for the past 10-15 years has been the best defenseman in the game. What else can you say about him? The guy just dominated while he played and he could probably still be playing right now, it's remarkable.

If you ever hear him speak he always gives credit to his teammates and the teams he's played on and it's truly remarkable to think of some of the players he's played with. So to win individual awards is something special but it also takes a special team. ... For Nick Lidstrom to win the Norris that many times, you know he's a tremendous hockey player but we all know he played with some great players and he'll be the first person to tell you that.

P.K. SUBBAN | Montreal Canadiens Defenseman
Norris Trophy Recipient, 2013

"

Obviously, he was one of the most consistent defensemen, but probably one of the toughest guys to go one-on-one with because of his stick and how he always poke-checked you. You couldn't get around him so you had to try to put it by him or put it into his feet but that didn't work half the time, either.

As a forward he was frustrating as heck, he was just phenomenal. You'd try to get around him and he would poke-check you at the blue line and the coach is all pissed off at you. Just things like how he ran the power play and his leadership skills and his consistency each and every year with his plus/minus.

He was just an honest defenseman, who played hard and wasn't doing anything stupid out there to try and hurt anybody. He was just very respectful. Look at what his record was all about. Just one of the best defensemen in the league for the longest time, so obviously, you guys were very fortunate to have him here in Detroit.

"

DOUG GILMOUR | NHL Center, 1983-2003
2011 HOF Inductee

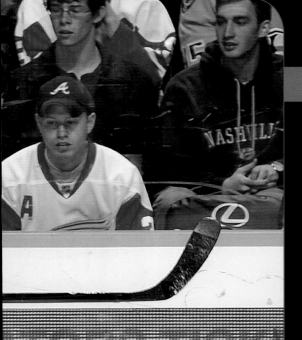

coach against because you could never get to Nicklas Lidstrom," Los Angeles Kings coach Darryl Sutter said.

Between the boards or in the dressing room, Lidstrom was a combination of high performance and low maintenance. "He was almost like a machine that tuned itself," former Detroit coach Dave Lewis said. "You didn't have to change the oil or anything. He was like a Swedish-built Volvo."

Lidstrom's place in the Detroit dressing room was easy to spot, and not because of his name plate over the stall. It was immaculate. All the pads hung up properly, skates positioned on their hooks, the helmet squarely situated on the shelf – a place for everything, and everything in its place.

Players can be demanding in their game-day needs, but Wings equipment manager Paul Boyer, whose job it is to oversee the team's gear, agreed that Lidstrom was absolutely wonderful to deal with. "He's perfect," Boyer said. "The best-ever. Talk about low-maintenance. I can't remember the last time he broke a stick. You'd go to his stall, all the stuff was in place."

Osgood thinks that taking care of his own business in terms of prepping and maintaining his gear was just another element of Lidstrom's uniqueness, an extension of what made him such a dominant performer.

"He wasn't flashy, but if you watched him during a game, he was Mr. Perfect," Osgood said. "He rarely made a mistake. He played effortlessly.

"Scott Niedermayer skated effortlessly, Nick did everything effortlessly. It's hard to explain. A perfect player – that would be a good way to put it."

The accomplishments on Lidstrom's resume are many. Both The Sporting News and Sports Illustrated named him NHL player of the decade in 2009. The Hockey News named him the best European player in NHL history.

He's the only player in NHL history to win 900 regular-season games with his team and his 1,564 regular-season games are a record for a one-team NHL player. His career plus-minus of plus-450 was the highest of any player who played in the NHL during Lidstrom's

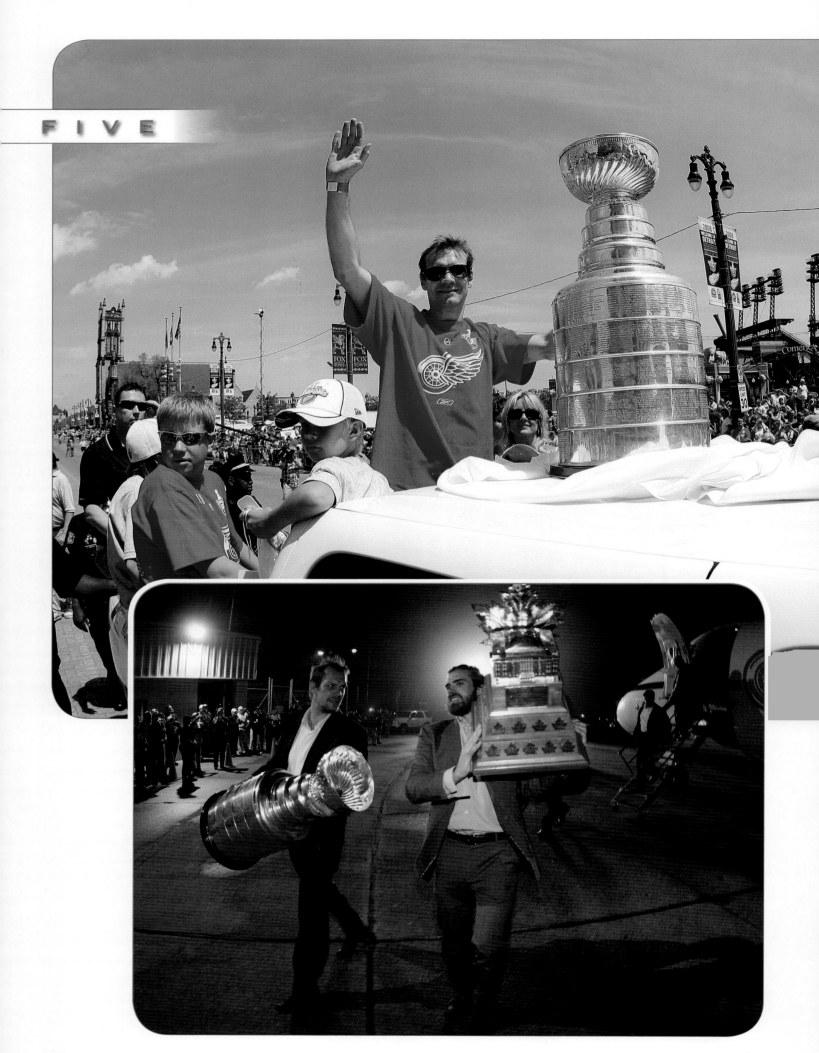

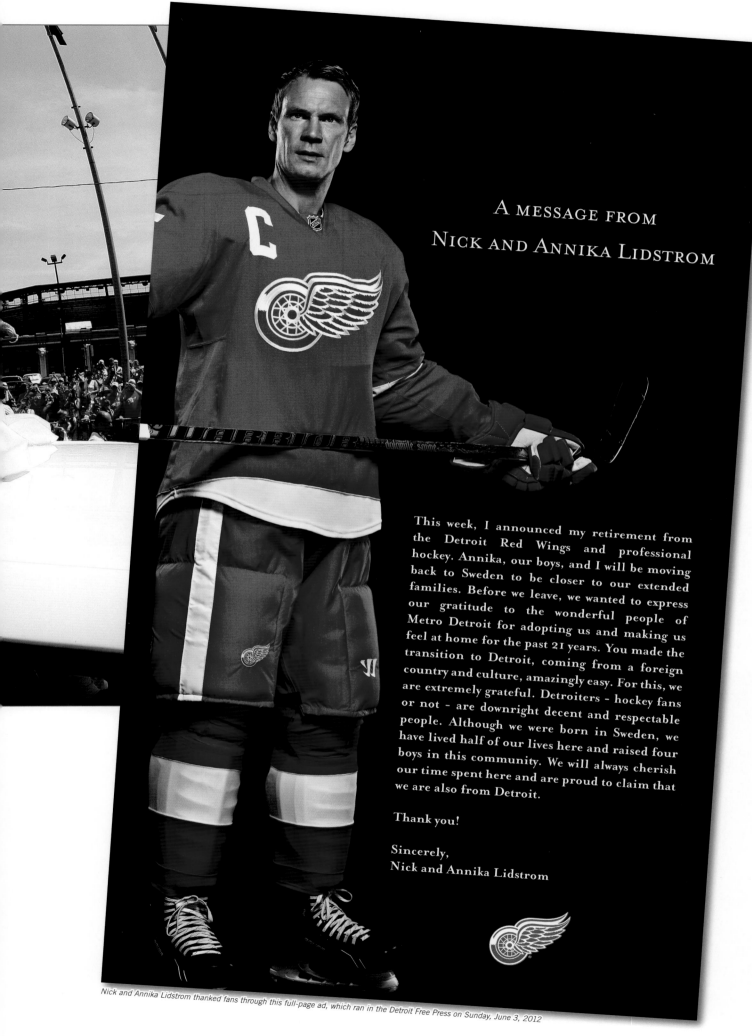

A MESSAGE FROM
NICK AND ANNIKA LIDSTROM

This week, I announced my retirement from the Detroit Red Wings and professional hockey. Annika, our boys, and I will be moving back to Sweden to be closer to our extended families. Before we leave, we wanted to express our gratitude to the wonderful people of Metro Detroit for adopting us and making us feel at home for the past 21 years. You made the transition to Detroit, coming from a foreign country and culture, amazingly easy. For this, we are extremely grateful. Detroiters - hockey fans or not - are downright decent and respectable people. Although we were born in Sweden, we have lived half of our lives here and raised four boys in this community. We will always cherish our time spent here and are proud to claim that we are also from Detroit.

Thank you!

Sincerely,
Nick and Annika Lidstrom

Nick and Annika Lidstrom thanked fans through this full-page ad, which ran in the Detroit Free Press on Sunday, June 3, 2012

"My D partner is the best D-man in the world," explained Ian White, who paired with Lidstrom for much of the 2011-12 season, Lidstrom's farewell NHL campaign.

The way he carried himself with similar class around close friends or strangers was another Lidstrom trait that even the all-time greats admired. "He's the perfect gentleman," Red Wings legend Gordie Howe said of Lidstrom.

Impressed as they were by his incomparable skills, those who played alongside Lidstrom were equally awed at his never-swaying temperament.

"I never saw him slam a gate, break a stick, throw a water bottle or raise his voice," Wings forward Daniel Cleary said. "His attitude, it was really amazing. You hope your kids grow up to be someone like him.

"I've never had more respect for a person at the NHL level. It was humbling to be around him. How he went about things, on and off the ice, I don't know if there was a thing Nick couldn't do. Well, maybe fighting."

And, apparently, golfing. But even that great equalizer, a sport that's caused the calmest of sorts to lose their cool on the links, never fazed Lidstrom.

"He doesn't even get mad when he plays golf," Osgood said. "And he's not a good golfer."

Seeking to recall a time when they saw Lidstrom get perplexed, his friends and teammates are at a loss. "I have a tough time thinking of anything that made him nervous," Detroit captain Henrik Zetterberg said. "Probably when he plays me on the golf course, that's when he gets nervous."

Actually, Lidstrom allowed there was a moment when his nerves nearly got the better

PLUS+

Lidstrom recorded the only hat-trick of his career during a 5-2 victory over the St. Louis Blues on Dec. 15, 2010. He joined Mathieu Schneider and Reed Larson as the only Detroit defensemen to record a three-goal game, but at 40 years and 210 days of age, he was the oldest NHL defenseman to record a hat-trick and the oldest NHLer to record his first hat-trick.

When you play as many teams and as many people there are a lot of great hockey players, but Nick Lidstrom always being one of the top guys, a good friend, a good human being and a combination of a good player and a good man who became an elite player, one of the best in the history of the hockey game.

Everybody told us we have no chance to beat Philly, especially with (Eric) Lindros and all of their top guys. The people who said so were wrong because the hockey game is played by the brain, by the skill, and by the heart, and not so much the size. It was fun to watch how Nick Lidstrom and Vladimir Konstantinov was and the other guys control those games and create a big celebration for Detroit for many years.

VIACHESLAV FETISOV | NHL Defenseman, 1989-98
2001 HOF Inductee

+PLUS

Lidstrom returned home to play for his hometown team Vasteras during the 1994-95 NHL lockout.

of him. "The most nervous I've ever been was when we were at the White House (in 2008 after winning the Stanley Cup)," Lidstrom said. "Giving a speech in front of the president (George W. Bush), that was nerve-racking."

Oh, and there's one other thing that leaves him a bit uncertain about the outcome – when his best friend, former Wings teammate Tomas Holmstrom, wants to get behind the wheel of their golf cart.

"That makes us all nervous," Zetterberg said.

At home in Vasteras, Lidstrom is a legend, but you'd never know it if you ran across him. St. Louis Blues forward Patrik Berglund, who's also from Vasteras, remembered sharing summer ice time with the town's local hero as they sought to stay in shape for the NHL season.

"He's very easy going, a very calm guy," said Berglund, whose father was Lidstrom's teammate in Vasteras. "He's quiet, but he's

very serious in everything he does. He's like a regular guy you know, but he was also the best defenseman in the world."

Lidstrom admitted that he often has to explain it to others when he's upset about something. "I don't show my emotions as much as other people," Lidstrom said. "I can lose my temper without other people knowing it."

Holmstrom insists he knows only one other person as calm and collected as Lidstrom – his grandfather. "In all the years I've known Nick, I've maybe heard him raise his voice three times," Holmstrom said. "My grandpa's calmer than Nick, but he's in his 80s."

Holmstrom remembered how Lidstrom took him under his wing when he first arrived in Detroit in the fall of 1996. "He's my best friend and he took care of me my first year," Holmstrom recalled. "He helped me get a car, a place. He showed me the ropes."

Lidstrom is such a hero in his homeland that during Detroit's 2008 visit to the U.S. Capitol, he and the Wings' other Swedes were

feted at the Swedish embassy. In 2009, the Wings opened the regular season with two games in Stockholm against St. Louis.

"The only reason we went was because of No. 5 and the rest of our Swedish players," said Detroit general manager Ken Holland, never a fan of playing NHL games in Europe. "I knew how much it would mean to Nick to play at home."

Lidstrom purchased 40 tickets for friends and family who got the chance to see him play in his homeland. "It's another thing you can look back at, having the chance to play with

the Wings in Sweden in front of your c fans," he said. "It's something I never thou would happen."

While in Sweden, Lidstrom was nam Ambassador of Honor for his home county Dalarna. It's a rare award. Lidstrom was o the second person so honored. The other w singer Kris Kristofferson, whose grandfat emigrated to the U.S. from the same coun

Plenty of off-ice honors came Lidstror way in Michigan as well. In 2006, he serv as grand marshal for America's Thanksgiv Parade in Detroit. In the spring of 20 Michigan International Speedway invi Lidstrom to serve as honorary pace car dri for its June NASCAR Sprint Cup race.

Lidstrom, who turned laps between 12 150 m.p.h., was impressed. "These drive they're very much athletes, with what th have to do in the heat, the focus a concentration they need to drive at the spee they're asked to travel for 2-3 hours," he sa "The speed I was going, I thought that w very fast, and it's nowhere near how fast th

BACK STORY

Detroit's 20-Year Men

When he took the ice for his first shift of the 2011-12 NHL season, Lidstrom joined an exclusive club that holds a unique tradition within the Motor City's sporting landscape. He became the sixth athlete to play 20 or more seasons exclusively with a Detroit team in one of the four big-league sports – NHL, NFL, NBA and Major League Baseball.

Lidstrom was the third Red Wing to achieve this unique feat, joining two previous Red Wings captains – Steve Yzerman (22 seasons) and Alex Delvecchio (24 seasons).

Playing in an era of unrestricted free agency and salary caps, Lidstrom admitted he wasn't expecting to play his entire NHL career as a Red Wing. "I didn't see myself staying here that long, especially back in the '90s when we saw a lot more trades, a lot more players moving," he said. "I didn't see that happening at all when I first came into the league.

"We've seen the last few years, guys signing long-term contracts that could be a hint that they're going to stay with one team for a long time, but there was still no guarantee that it was going to happen."

On Feb. 12, 2012, a 4-3 victory over the Philadelphia Flyers at Joe Louis Arena, Lidstrom played in his 1,550th NHL game, surpassing Delvecchio's NHL mark for the most games played by a player whose entire career was spent with one team.

"It means a lot to me to have been able to play with one team throughout my career and moving up, especially moving ahead of such a legend as Alex Delvecchio," Lidstrom said.

Delvecchio was proud to pass on his mark to a fellow Red Wing. "He's a great hockey player," he said. "To be truthful, I didn't even know I had any record for playing games. All I wanted to do was play hockey. But I can't think of a better person to beat it than Nick.

"He was a good player. He wasn't that rough and tough on the ice, but he handled himself, checked well, and had a great shot. He was just a leader out there."

Detroit's 20-year, one-team legacy extends to baseball, where both outfielder Al Kaline (21) and shortstop Alan Trammell (20) were two-decade players with the Detroit Tigers. On the gridiron, kicker Jason Hanson played 21 seasons, all with the NFL's Detroit Lions.

"I guess I'm in some nice company then," Lidstrom said.

After Detroit, Chicago lists four 20-season men – Stan Mikita (22) of the Blackhawks, and Ted Lyons (21), Red Faber (20), and Luke Appling (20) of the White Sox. Montreal (Jean Beliveau 20 and Henri Richard 20, of the Canadiens) and Baltimore (Brooks Robinson 23 and Cal Ripken, Jr. 21, of the Orioles) are the only other cities to sport more than one of these unique athletes.

CONSUMATE PRO

"Drafting an All-Star team against him is definitely up there on my career list of honors I've been fortunate to be part of. A moment and memory for myself and my family I'll never forget. Like I said to be alongside a Hall of Famer and someone with the storied career he has was special for me and you know, very fun weekend for sure.

"It was fun, you weren't going to go around with just any player, it was an All-Star Game. That was the best part about it. We tried to make it as fun and entertaining for the fans as we could. It was Nick and Marty St. Louis and Pat Kane for them that were kind of making the picks, and myself, Mike Green and Ryan Kesler kind of the younger guys on the other side. I think both sides had fun with it, just enjoyed the whole process and tried to make it entertaining and I think we succeeded in making it pretty cool."

ERIC STAAL
Carolina Hurricanes Captain

Salutes Nicklas Lidstrom

Count on Us

In 2011, when the NHL changed its All-Star Game format and allowed the players involved to draft the two teams, such was the respect around the league for Lidstrom that his NHL peers voted him captain of one of the teams.

"I think Nick is one of those guys, when you have a chance to be on a team with a guy like that, it helps you to grow as a hockey player, and as a person as well," said fellow Swedish blue-liner and former Detroit teammate Niklas Kronwall. "Growing up in Sweden, he was the guy everybody looked up to as a role model."

Later in 2011, the road leading up to Novi Ice Arena, where Lidstrom's sons played their youth hockey, was renamed Nicklas Lidstrom Drive, something that clearly meant as much to him as his all-star captaincy.

"I was truly honored to be recognized like that and to have a street named after me," he said. "All four of my kids played hockey through that association."

Bob Tripi, who served as a Novi Youth Hockey Association executive, remembered that there wasn't anything Lidstrom wasn't willing to do to help the organization out.

"Yes, Nick was a professional hockey player, but he always had time for people," Tripi said. "I actually remember one time when we had our annual Hockey Day celebration and he

volunteered to sit at a table to sign autographs for free. And Nick's support for youth hockey was unbelievable – from helping coach on the ice to donating his jerseys to raise money."

When Lidstrom opted to call it quits following the 2011-12 season at the age of 41, his reasons were as simple and sound as his game.

"It's something that I'm proud of, to be able to play at a high level for a long period of time," he said. "I know how much fun it is playing, but I also know what it takes to be there and that's something I can't do – be up to that level of play where I want to be.

"Retiring allowed me to walk away from the game with pride rather than have the game walk away from me."

Wings coach Mike Babcock felt Lidstrom established a different standard of excellence by which he's judged. "He's the best player I've ever coached, by far," Babcock said. "He was absolutely beyond professional. How can you do everything right, all the time? I've never seen anything, anyone like him.

"Nick is an example to everyone in the profession. To me, simple is the best. He made the first simple play over and over again. He didn't try to be on the highlight reel.

"Who was a better player? I don't mean defenseman, I mean, who was a better player than Nick Lidstrom in this league?"

Even those who opposed him couldn't find joy in an NHL without Lidstrom.

"You can't hate that guy," Anaheim Ducks forward Teemu Selanne said. "He was so classy, played so fair and he has no enemies."

It was left to Red Wings owner Mike Ilitch to attempt to put into words what Lidstrom meant to Detroit.

"Nick has been a Rock of Gibraltar," Ilitch said. "He's been a solid leader. He's been professional and a good citizen. He's never done anything to hurt his reputation or the reputation of his team."

A perfect description of the perfect human. 5

We were neighbors, we lived in the same subdivision in Northville. Coming from Hawaii I didn't know much about hockey and learning about the tradition of the Red Wings and learning about the tradition of the captains, I think when I met Nick he had an 'A' on his jersey. I met him through a couple of the other guys and the nicest guy the first time I met him I think was at like a Cup party or something.

I have a different respect for hockey players as it is just because, I can relate to other professional sports but a hockey team is totally different. They welcomed me in, nobody had an ego, nothing at all and then I did kind of my history and looked up and read about Nick more and thought, 'Wow this guy is pretty great and defensive player of the year.' So I have a different respect for him. He's the ultimate symbol of professionalism, I mean, because on and off the ice and he was so level headed, he never got too far ahead of himself, always kept himself in good shape. I wouldn't see him over the summer he'd be back in Sweden and he'd get back and he'd look the same and he'd be in top physical condition.

DOMINIC RAIOLA | Detroit Lions Center

5

FIVE

Captain Reflections

Red Wings' captains from
yesterday and today weigh in
on Lidstrom's contributions

He's just good at everything. He doesn't have a weakness. He's a good skater. He's good with the puck. He's intelligent. He plays his position very well. Probably the most frustrating thing about playing against him would be just his uncanny ability to hold onto the puck and at the very right moment make an excellent pass. It's frustrating for a guy forechecking him because you know you have to get there, but as soon as you get there he's going to pass the puck off and just slip by your check.

It's hard to find, particularly defensemen, that can step in right away and play and make an impact, and he was able to do that. So our team, I think, we quickly moved up in the standings because we got players like Nicklas.

STEVE YZERMAN NHL Center, 1983-2006
Conn Smythe Trophy Recipient, 1998

C RED WINGS CAPTAIN • 1978-79

"I picture back, and he might have been the most intelligent player that I've seen in the NHL. He had the ability to read the plays and he just knew what to do in every situation whether it was offensively or defensively. In your mind, you can't picture him making any bad plays. He always seemed to make the right play over and over and over again. It's just amazing to think back to how few mistakes he really did make.

"He wasn't a guy who was going end to end with the puck and making plays that stand out, but he slowly and methodically through the course of the game he made play after play after play. There are very few guys who are your best offensive player and best defensive player at the same time. It's a really, really rare combination at such a high level, but he was. He played in every situation, power play, killed penalties against the opposing team's best players shift after shift. To watch him play was truly amazing, and the closer you watched him the more you understood what he did."

PAUL WOODS
NHL Left Wing, 1977-84

C RED WINGS CAPTAIN • 1975-77

"I think because guys like Denis Potvin and Serge Savard and Rick Lapointe all played at the same time Bobby Orr did they kind of took a back seat. If they were playing today, we'd be talking about them the same we are about Lidstrom and Orr. But Lidstrom was at a time that there's no question he was the best, there was no argument, the second or third guys weren't as close as say Savard or those guys were to Orr. A guy like Lidstrom, with his skating ability and his ability to see the ice and everything like that, there's no question he's far and above anybody playing the game right now.

"It's just wonderful to be able to look at an athlete who both on and off the ice just carried himself the way that we all expect our role models to be and Lidstrom is certainly a role model, not only here in Canada but across the whole world."

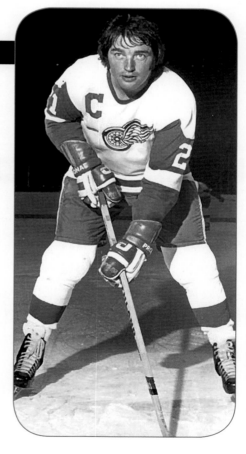

DANNY GRANT
NHL Right Wing, 1965-79

C RED WINGS CAPTAIN • 1956-58

I never actually saw him play except on TV and so on but from what I saw on TV, Nick seemed to be always effective and he must've been in order to win the Norris Trophy so many times.

I think Nick winning the Norris seven times is just great. The Red Wings had some great years and so did Nick, I guess, so you know you depend on the voters, how they vote so you just go out and play your game. You're part of a team and you do the best you can and you're trying to get your team to win. You don't think about the Norris Trophy or anything, you just think about winning, winning the Stanley Cup and how you help the team to win. So I don't think you think about the Norris Trophy, I think you just go out and do the best job you can like Nick did.

RED KELLY | NHL Defenseman, 1947-67
Norris Trophy Recipient, 1954

C RED WINGS CAPTAIN • 1976-77

"In the Red Wings' weight room, along the top of the wall there's a head and shoulders picture of all the ex-captains so it's easy to understand that Nick and other players may know who I am. So when I'm in Detroit or when Detroit comes to Calgary they let me go right into the dressing room to say 'Hi' to the guys. I know Kenny Holland well and I know Jim Bedard well and the training staff and so forth, so when I walked in one day a few years ago and they'd taken something to Nick Lidstrom to sign and he looked up and he said, 'Oh, hi, Mr. Polonich.' I thought, 'Wow! Nick Lidstrom, the Norris Trophy winner, calling me Mr. Polonich? Wow!' But having read quotes from Mike Babcock and others, what a consummate professional Nick is, again, it's just a testament to his greatness."

DENNIS POLONICH
NHL Center/Right Wing, 1974-83

C RED WINGS CAPTAIN • 1973-74, 1978-79

"Obviously he was a great player. I don't like to use the phrase 'quiet good,' but that's kind of what he was. He wasn't an end-to-ender like Bobby Orr or Paul Coffey but at the end of the night he was plus-4, had a goal and a couple of assists and nobody could score when he was on the ice. He just did things under the radar so to speak, that's my impression of him.

"If you watch him play, he never really ran and crashed into guys, he always played the angles. In other words, you never got around him. When you thought you got around him you looked up and you're in the corner, you just couldn't get around him because he always had the angles."

NICK LIBETT
NHL Left Wing, 1967-81

C RED WINGS CAPTAIN • 1977-79

"He was one of the cleanest defensemen I've ever seen with all of his talent. I'll put it this way, and I think this will give you my feelings: if I was picking an All-Star team from the NHL today and I picked two defensemen it'd be Bobby Orr and Nick Lidstrom.

"Nick was a little more defensive than Orr and I don't think he was as explosive as Orr was. He didn't play with the toughness that Orr did, but as far as being smart and not being dirty he was always in position. You hardly ever caught him out of position. He was a class act on and off the ice."

DENNIS HEXTALL
NHL Left Wing, 1968-80

C RED WINGS CAPTAIN • 1973-74

"He was so good, so smart that he made everything he did look easy. And he did it all pretty much with his head because he didn't play a physical game. From a thinking standpoint, he was three steps ahead of other players. He was way ahead of the game.

"Over the 20 years that he was here he was always very cordial to me and always had time to say 'Hello.' I was amazed, really, that he went about his business in the National Hockey League as quietly as he did. For sure, he could have been nicknamed the Quiet Man. He never said much, rarely raised his voice, rarely got mad, an incredible personality to be as great a player as he was for as long as he was in the game."

MICKEY REDMOND
NHL Right Wing, 1967-76

C RED WINGS CAPTAIN • 1975-76

"His record speaks for itself. It was an amazing run he had and to stay with one team is pretty nice. His longevity it was kind of the dream, it's in the dream world. That doesn't happen and yet it did for him because he put the right things together I guess. Had the right attitude, came around at the right time to the right organization.

"I thought Nick played defense the way I thought it should be played. He was very strong defensively and a factor offensively. I think there probably were similar players when I played. I think maybe one of the best defensemen ever that I played with was Doug Harvey, maybe one of the best defensemen that ever played the game that would be in that same class. Nick would be in that same league as him."

TERRY HARPER
NHL Defenseman, 1962-81

RED WINGS CAPTAIN · 1962-73

"He was a great defenseman, a great leader. I think he had a lot of self-confidence, and to me, it looked like he settled the play down, he took charge. They would get into that (defensive) zone with everybody running around and all of that and when he got the puck he slowed the whole pace up, got the guys organized, and then one pass and they were out of the zone.

It was so nice to see a guy like him do so much for the Red Wings, regardless of him breaking a record that I didn't even know I had because we had such bad years. But to see him do it, he just conducts himself so professionally, takes it in stride and that's the type of guy he is.

It's really an honor to have your number, or your sweater, retired and hanging from the rafters and Nick certainly belongs up there. I think in the modern era with Stevie and him, they're well deserving of being up there, and I think we'll probably see some more up there."

ALEX DELVECCHIO | NHL Left Wing/Center 1950-74

RED WINGS CAPTAIN • 1952-56

"

The perfect gentleman and that's what he is. The greatest compliment that I can pay to him is you hear about Bobby Orr of the modern era, you hear about Doug Harvey of my era and Nick goes with both of those guys as one of the greatest defensemen ever to play. He comes into the room and he dresses then he goes out and plays. He comes back in, he showers then he leaves, and if you don't look at the stats you wouldn't even know he was in the building. That's just how great he is.

I know that he's a man of his word. When he told you he'd do something he did it. His greatness didn't screw up his head. He's very thankful for what he has in this world and he appreciates people's time and he wants to be respected by people. He's just a pleasure to be around.

"

TED LINDSAY | NHL Left Wing, 1944-60, 1964-65
1966 HOF Inductee

C RED WINGS CAPTAIN · 1980-81

"In my era there weren't too many 20-year veterans that started in 1970 and went through to 1990. The longevity just wasn't there for my generation for some reason. But to be honest with you, I don't think Nick got the recognition that he deserves.

"I know when Mr. Lindsay gave me the 'C' you were suppose to be a team leader and more of a liaison between the players and the management than today's captains who are probably dealing with a whole lot more pressure. While I don't know a lot about Nick I know from what I've read and the little I've seen on TV that he had an amazing career in Detroit."

ERROL THOMPSON
NHL Left Wing, 1970-81

C RED WINGS CAPTAIN · 1973-74

"The thing about Nick is that he did everything well and he did everything right, and to me, every drill was, 'We have to do this right,' and he did it right, and usually better than most players. So it was no surprise in games when you saw him make those perfect passes or be in the right position in a defensive situation. He did all of those things in practice. I was really impressed with him on the ice with all the drills, and you know here's a guy, he could coast through training camp, but he never did. It seemed like he was trying to make the team rather than here's a guy that was one of the best players on the team. That was the kind of effort he gave."

RED BERENSON
NHL Center, 1961-78

C RED WINGS CAPTAIN · 1973-74

"He was similar to Bobby Orr, he controlled the play, he kept the game at his pace you know that's the way the game was played was at his pace and he just anticipated so well and you know he just handled the puck unbelievably well without being a physical guy. He was never really a physical guy he just played his position.

"I guess I'm saying what most people would say, he was just an outstanding player and fun to watch because you know he just did everything so easy. The game came so easy to him it appeared. I'm not saying it did, but it appeared that it did. You know what I mean? He knocked down passes out of the air, put the puck up on everybody's stick and these guys never had to break stride, offensively he was just outstanding."

LARRY JOHNSTON
NHL Defenseman, 1967-77

C RED WINGS CAPTAIN • 1979-80

"Once I went to Europe I pretty much lost contact with the NHL and what was going on there. Nick came in after my time, but I certainly heard of him over the last couple of years and what he's done. I never met him, but his accomplishments speak volumes of the type of person that he was, I mean, being a defenseman and winning four Stanley Cups and seven Norris Trophies is unbelievable and puts him in the top echelon of hockey players and defensemen."

DALE McCOURT
NHL Center, 1977-84

C RED WINGS CAPTAIN • 1982-86

"I met Nick a couple of times and we talked mostly about Stevie (Yzerman) because he came after Stevie and I was before Stevie as captain. So we had some nice conversations in that regard. ... What a remarkable career. It just tells you about the character that he has: He came to work and did his job, led by example and I think he was a special player.

"He had an ability to box out individuals because of his size. Then he had an active stick and the way he positioned his stick, once he had a winger in a situation

to the outside going toward the net, if you didn't get there early on him you had no play on him. When you talk about positional hockey that was his game, plus he was a great skater.

"To be the elite player and leader that he was he had great dedication, work ethic and was the complete team player. From what I understood, he was a quiet leader. As a former captain, there are vocal leaders, and there are quiet leaders, who lead by example, and that's what Nick Lidstrom was."

DANNY GARE
NHL Right Wing, 1974-87

He was always steady. You put him on the ice and you knew what you were going to get back. He was as vital to the Red Wings as Red Kelly was to us; pretty strong but could always hold back when he had to. Nick always had everything to give and you could see it on film when he would get inside the shooter and the goaltender, he was always in between them.

GORDIE HOWE NHL Right Wing, 1946-71, 1979-80
1972 HOF Inductee

We all get hurt. We all have injuries. I was lucky that I never got to that point because certain players get hit hard, a knee goes here, a shoulder goes there. It looks like he managed pretty well. I'm sure he had many bumps and bruises, but I never heard of him missing a long time. That's luck, that's pure luck. I know he got hit, we all get hit and we all get hurt, but his longevity was amazing.

Nick played the game the way it should be played. It was very simple. You can talk all you want about being physical and so on, but when you start playing the game you don't think about being physical. You think about chasing the puck and playing with the puck, taking it away from people and that's basically what he did. Nick Lidstrom was smart enough to poke-check, he was the best of all-time. You didn't have to worry about going to the corners and getting hit. You only had to worry about him making you look like a fool when he took the puck away from you.

What an accomplishment. I'm very proud for a guy like that and a Red Wing like that. He had his time and now it's up to someone else.

MARCEL DIONNE   NHL Center, 1971-89
1992 HOF Inductee

C RED WINGS CAPTAIN • 1977-78

There was Bobby and Denis and Nick. Man, was Nick one helluva player. He's a wonderful guy, a perfect gentleman and everything I thought he would be when I met him. But just his ability to advance the puck, one pass, two passes; the guy knew what the hell he was doing. Man, he could move the puck. That first pass out of your own end is critical but the nice thing about Nick was that he was durable too. He reminded me of Denis a little bit when he would shoot it from the blue line. … Just can't say enough nice things about him.

DAN MALONEY
NHL Left Wing 1970-82

C RED WINGS CAPTAIN • 1981-82

"When you talk about Nick and defensemen who are either defense-oriented or offense-oriented, I think he was well-balanced. He wasn't little, he was a good size, strong, offensively good, defensively great. I think he played on some very good Detroit Red Wings teams, but I'll tell you what, gosh, if you had to put a guy out at the last two minutes to protect the lead I don't know who else you'd pick above him.

"He really scored some nice goals, some big key goals. He'd come up with the big play once in a while; I wouldn't rule him out. And he's the last guy to talk about himself, too. He's a class guy."

REED LARSON
NHL Defenseman, 1976-90

C RED WINGS CAPTAIN • 1973-74

"To win the Norris Trophy that many times like Nick did you pretty much have to be a leader back there. You're kind of like the quarterback because that first pass up to the forwards is so crucial.

"I played five seasons for Toe Blake (in Montreal) and the importance of making a clean pass out of our zone was practically beat into us every day. He was so fond of Bobby Orr and the way he skated, he wanted us to be more like him but when Orr wound up I backed up. He was such a good skater, like Nick, who was able to calm everything down back there with his smooth skating and his leadership ability."

TED HARRIS
NHL Defenseman, 1963-75

C RED WINGS CAPTAIN • 2013-present

It was an honor for me to take over the captaincy after Nick. Since I got here he was probably the guy who helped me off and on the most. Once I got a little more comfortable here he was the guy that I kept learning from and he's the 'Perfect Human Being' as I used to say and I'm still saying. He was always the guy when you needed him he was always there. He was rarely injured and always played the best in our most important games. I learned a lot from him with the way he led the team, the way he showed it on the ice. He was always there for the guys and always helped me a lot.

It doesn't matter what you say you always have to go out there and show it, and I think if I have to take one thing from him, it's that he showed me how to do that.

HENRIK ZETTERBERG | NHL Left Wing, 2002-present
Conn Smythe Trophy Recipient, 2008

5 FIVE

By the Numbers

Statistical breakdowns and a timeline of Nick's stellar career

1970

Apr. 28   Lidstrom is born in Vasteras, Sweden

1988

Apr. 9-17   Played for Sweden in IIHF European Junior Championships in Czechoslovakia.

1989

June 17   Selected 53rd overall by Detroit in NHL entry draft held at the Met Center in Bloomington, Minnesota.

1990

Jan. 4   Played for Sweden in IIHF World Junior Hockey Championships in Helsinki, Finland. Collected three goals and three assists in seven games and was named one of Sweden's top players.

1991

May 2   Scored two goals in an 8-4 win over the United States at the IIHF World Championships in Turku, Finland.

May 4   Helped Sweden win the IIHF World Hockey Championships. Led Swedish defensemen with six points in 10 games.

May 19   Signed his first contract with the Red Wings.

Aug. 31   Played for Sweden in the Canada Cup, paired on defense with Swedish legend Borje Salming.

Oct. 3   Made his NHL debut in a 3-3 overtime tie with the Blackhawks at Chicago Stadium.

Oct. 5   Collected his first NHL point, an assist on a goal by Jimmy Carson in an 8-5 loss to Toronto at Maple Leaf Gardens. He also assisted on a goal by Steve Yzerman for the first multi-point game of his NHL career.

Oct. 17   Beat future teammate Vincent Riendeau for his first NHL goal in a 6-3 win over the St. Louis Blues at Joe Louis Arena. Added a pair of assists for his first career three-point game.

Nov. 7   A four-point game in a 10-3 rout of the St. Louis Blues at Joe Louis Arena, included Lidstrom's first two-goal game, both tallies coming against goalie Pat Jablonski.

1992

Feb. 27   An assist on a Brad McCrimmon goal in a 4-2 loss to the Blackhawks at Chicago Stadium gave Lidstrom 42 assists, breaking the club record for a rookie defenseman previously established by Reed Larson in 1977-78.

Apr. 14   Set up a Gerard Gallant goal during a 7-4 win over the Minnesota North Stars at the Met Center for his 49th assist of the season, tying Marcel Dionne's club rookie record set in 1971-72. Lidstrom's 60 points also tied Reed Larson's mark for a Red Wings' rookie defenseman.

Apr. 18   Made Stanley Cup debut as Detroit lost 4-3 to the Minnesota North Stars at Joe Louis Arena.

April 22   Scored his first Stanley Cup goal against goalie Jon Casey in a 5-4 overtime win over the Minnesota North Stars at the Met Center.

May 5   Announced as a finalist for the Calder Trophy as NHL rookie of the year along with Pavel Bure of the Vancouver Canucks and Tony Amonte of the New York Rangers.

June 16   Finished second behind Pavel Bure of the Vancouver Canucks in Calder Trophy balloting for the NHL's rookie of the year.

June 19   Named to the NHL's All-Rookie Team.

Nov. 17   Enjoyed a three-assist game in a 5-4 win over the Chicago Blackhawks at Joe Louis Arena.

1993

April 1   Lidstrom's second goal of the game against goalie Ed Belfour in a 3-1 win over the Blackhawks at Chicago Stadium is his 100th NHL point.

Nick's Regular-Season Teammates

PLAYER	GAMES
Kris Draper	1107
Tomas Holmstrom	992
Steve Yzerman	907
Kirk Maltby	884
Sergei Fedorov	816
Pavel Datsyuk	715
Brendan Shanahan	703
Darren McCarty	648
Henrik Zetterberg	645
Mathieu Dandenault	604
Vyacheslav Kozlov	596
Chris Chelios	560
Chris Osgood	551
Martin Lapointe	540
Igor Larionov	533
Brett Hull	492
Daniel Cleary	472
Johan Franzen	449
Niklas Kronwall	447
Vladimir Konstantinov	440
Valtteri Filppula	418
Doug Brown	415
Jiri Hudler	385
Brett Lebda	312
Larry Murphy	309
Jiri Fischer	299
Keith Primeau	299
Brad Stuart	288
Brian Rafalski	287
Andreas Lilja	285
Jason Williams	271
Ray Sheppard	269
Aaron Ward	265
Mikael Samuelsson	264
Boyd Devereaux	252
Dino Ciccarelli	250
Shawn Burr	248
Darren Helm	238
Bob Rouse	236
Todd Bertuzzi	232
Mathieu Schneider	226
Paul Coffey	225
Bob Probert	209
Jonathan Ericsson	207
Drew Miller	201
Justin Abdelkader	198
Viacheslav Fetisov	196
Steve Duchesne	194

PLAYER	GAMES
Jimmy Howard	185
Dallas Drake	178
Greg Johnson	178
Manny Legace	176
Tomas Kopecky	172
Dominik Hasek	170
Tim Cheveldae	169
Jason Woolley	168
Brent Gilchrist	166
Luc Robitaille	159
Paul Ysebaert	159
Sheldon Kennedy	156
Robert Lang	154
Anders Eriksson	147
Yves Racine	141
Brad McCrimmon	139
Patrick Eaves	138
Gerard Gallant	136
Pat Verbeek	134
Joe Kocur	133
Tim Taylor	133
Jimmy Carson	132
Bob Errey	131
Jamie Pushor	129
Mike Sillinger	126
Steve Chiasson	123
Mark Howe	122
Maxim Kuznetsov	113
Stacy Roest	108
Todd Gill	102
Jakub Kindl	102
Mark Mowers	96
Curtis Joseph	92
Derek Meech	91
Mike Vernon	91
Kevin Miller	84
Terry Carkner	83
Mike Ramsey	77
Ruslan Salei	75
Yuri Butsayev	74
Jamie Macoun	74
Sean Avery	71
Dmitri Bykov	71
Marian Hossa	71
Marc Bergevin	70
Ray Whitney	66
Ian White	65
Danny Markov	64

PLAYER	GAMES
Jamie Rivers	63
Stu Grimson	62
Cory Emmerton	61
Brent Fedyk	61
Micah Aivazoff	59
Mike Knuble	59
Alan Kerr	58
Aaron Downey	55
Ville Leino	55
Brad Marsh	55
Ty Conklin	51
Matt Ellis	51
Yan Golubovsky	50
Jesse Wallin	47
Fredrik Olausson	46
Steve Thomas	43
Brad May	40
Mike Modano	40
Dennis Vial	36
Kevin Hodson	34
Darryl Laplante	34
Bobby Dollas	33
Josh Langfeld	33
Jan Mursak	33
Tomas Sandstrom	33
Bob Halkidis	32
Vincent Riendeau	32
Joey MacDonald	31
Darryl Bootland	28
Ken Wregget	28
Uwe Krupp	27
Doug Crossman	26
Patrick Boileau	25
Steve Konroyd	25
Brian MacLellan	23
Mark Hartigan	22
Jim Hiller	21
Marc Rodgers	21
Doug Janik	20
Norm Maracle	20
Gord Kruppke	19
John Ogrodnick	19
Jason York	19
Kyle Calder	17
Mike Krushelnyski	17
Kyle Quincey	17
Mike Commodore	16
Johan Garpenlov	16

PLAYER	GAMES
Cory Cross	15
Derian Hatcher	14
Bob Essensa	13
Petr Klima	13
Gustav Nyquist	13
Bob McGill	12
Wendel Clark	11
Greg Millen	10
Dmitri Mironov	10
Tomas Tatar	9
Jim Cummins	8
Anders Myrvold	8
Chris Conner	7
Troy Crowder	7
Mattias Ritola	7
Brad Norton	6
Fabian Brunnstrom	5
Matt Hussey	5
Marc Potvin	5
Nathan Robinson	5
Jiri Slegr	5
Chris Tancill	5
Joakim Andersson	4
Philippe Audet	4
Steve Maltais	4
Kris Newbury	4
Bill Ranford	4
Doug Houda	3
Peter Ing	3
Don MacLean	3
Ulf Samuelsson	3
Brendan Smith	3
Rick Zombo	3
Ryan Barnes	2
Mark Ferner	2
Marc Lamothe	2
Mark Major	2
Andrew McKim	2
Mark Pederson	2
Sergei Bautin	1
Allan Bester	1
Scott King	1
Ladislav Kohn	1
Thomas McCollum	1
Riley Sheahan	1
Wes Walz	1
B.J. Young	1

TIMELINE

1994 continued

Jan. 14 — Posted a career-best plus-seven rating during a 9-2 win over the Dallas Stars at Joe Louis Arena.

Apr. 14 — Finished season third in NHL with a plus-43 rating.

Apr. 26 — Scored two goals in Detroit's 6-4 victory over the San Jose Sharks at San Jose Arena in Game 5 of their opening round Stanley Cup series.

May 8 — Helped Sweden to a bronze medal at the World Hockey Championships in Italy. Scored a goal as the Swedes defeated the United States 7-2 in the bronze-medal game.

Oct. 27 — Joined his old Swedish team Vasteras during the NHL lockout.

1995

Jan. 24 — Scored twice against goalie Kirk McLean in a 6-3 victory over the Vancouver Canucks at Joe Louis Arena.

April 11 — Missed the first of five consecutive games due to a sore back, ending a consecutive games played streak of 274 that extended back to the beginning of Lidstrom's NHL career.

May 9 — Scored twice against goalie Andy Moog as Detroit downed the Dallas Stars 4-1 in Game 2 of their Stanley Cup opening-round series at Joe Louis Arena.

June 1 — Scored on Chicago's Ed Belfour 1:01 into overtime to give Detroit a 2-1 decision over the Blackhawks in the opening game of the Western Conference finals at Joe Louis Arena. It was the first Stanley Cup overtime goal scored by a Red Wings player in a game at Detroit since Jerry Melnyk scored against Toronto at Olympia Stadium on March 27, 1960.

June 22 — Recorded his 12th assist during a 5-2 loss to the New Jersey Devils at Meadowlands Arena in Game 3 of the Stanley Cup finals to tie the club record for assists by a defenseman in one playoff year.

Aug. 14 — Signed a four-year contract with the Red Wings.

Nov. 4 — Collected three assists in a 5-1 win over the Dallas Stars at Joe Louis Arena.

Nov. 17 — Recorded his 200th NHL point with an assist in a 5-4 win over the Edmonton Oilers at Joe Louis Arena.

Dec. 23 — Voted the NHL's most underrated player in a players' poll conducted by the Toronto Sun.

1996

Jan. 20 — Made his NHL All-Star Game debut, playing for the Western Conference in the 46th All-Star Game at Boston's FleetCenter.

Jan. 27 — Scored with 18 seconds left in regulation time to earn the Wings a 5-5 tie with the Chicago Blackhawks at the United Center.

Mar. 19 — Scored twice against goalie Felix Potvin in Detroit's 6-5 victory over the Toronto Maple Leafs at Joe Louis Arena.

Apr. 11 — Named to the Swedish roster for the 1996 World Cup of Hockey.

Apr. 12 — An assist in a 5-3 victory over the Chicago Blackhawks at Joe Louis Arena completed Lidstrom's season with a career-high 67 points.

Apr. 23 — Collected three assists as Detroit took a 4-1 decision from the Jets in Game 3 of their Stanley Cup opening-round playoff series at Winnipeg Arena.

May 5 — Scored twice against goalie Jon Casey as Detroit routed the St. Louis Blues 8-3 in Game 2 of their Western Conference semifinals series at Joe Louis Arena.

May 23 — Scored twice against Patrick Roy and added an assist as Detroit recorded a 6-4 win over the Colorado Avalanche in Game 3 of the Western Conference finals at McNichols Arena.

Aug. 26 — Tallied the first goal in World Cup of Hockey history, opening the scoring in Sweden's 6-1 triumph over Germany.

Nov. 21 — Scored twice in a span of 52 seconds during the opening period of

Nick's Playoff Teammates

PLAYER	GAMES	PLAYER	GAMES	PLAYER	GAMES	PLAYER	GAMES
Kris Draper	220	Andreas Lilja	47	Patrick Eaves	19	Steve Thomas	6
Tomas Holmstrom	178	Dominik Hasek	45	Tim Cheveldae	18	Cory Emmerton	5
Kirk Maltby	167	Larry Murphy	45	Danny Markov	18	Ville Leino	5
Darren McCarty	167	Todd Bertuzzi	44	Kyle Quincey	18	Jamie Pushor	5
Steve Yzerman	157	Ray Sheppard	42	Yves Racine	18	Ian White	5
Sergei Fedorov	155	Mike Vernon	42	Marc Bergevin	17	Dmitri Bykov	4
Pavel Datsyuk	126	Shawn Burr	41	Gerard Gallant	17	Mark Hartigan	4
Vyacheslav Kozlov	114	Brett Hull	39	Paul Ysebaert	17	Gustav Nyquist	4
Chris Osgood	108	Steve Duchesne	38	Todd Gill	16	Bill Ranford	4
Henrik Zetterberg	107	Jiri Fischer	38	Mark Howe	16	Mike Knuble	3
Brendan Shanahan	106	Joe Kocur	37	Sheldon Kennedy	14	Brad Marsh	3
Igor Larionov	105	Robert Lang	36	Pat Verbeek	14	Mark Mowers	3
Chris Chelios	101	Justin Abdelkader	35	Kyle Calder	13	Stacy Roest	3
Daniel Cleary	95	Mathieu Schneider	33	Stu Grimson	13	Bobby Dollas	2
Valtteri Filppula	89	Bob Errey	32	Curtis Joseph	13	Bob Essensa	2
Johan Franzen	86	Mike Ramsey	30	Petr Klima	13	Jim Hiller	2
Martin Lapointe	83	Aaron Ward	30	Derian Hatcher	12	Uwe Krupp	2
Vladimir Konstantinov	82	Dallas Drake	29	Tomas Kopecky	12	Norm Maracle	2
Viacheslav Fetisov	78	Brent Gilchrist	29	Ray Whitney	12	Mike Modano	2
Niklas Kronwall	77	Jimmy Howard	28	Jimmy Carson	11	Vincent Riendeau	2
Doug Brown	71	Luc Robitaille	27	Manny Legace	11	Jamie Rivers	2
Brad Stuart	70	Boyd Devereaux	26	Brad McCrimmon	11	Troy Crowder	1
Bob Rouse	67	Drew Miller	26	Ruslan Salei	11	Brent Fedyk	1
Mikael Samuelsson	67	Tim Taylor	26	Wendel Clark	10	Bob Halkidis	1
Mathieu Dandenault	64	Steve Chiasson	25	Alan Kerr	9	Kevin Hodson	1
Jiri Hudler	64	Bob Probert	25	Kevin Miller	9	Steve Konroyd	1
Darren Helm	63	Jamie Macoun	23	Ulf Samuelsson	9	Derek Meech	1
Brian Rafalski	63	Jason Williams	23	Mike Krushelnyski	8	John Ogrodnick	1
Brett Lebda	60	Anders Eriksson	21	Bob McGill	8	Marc Potvin	1
Keith Primeau	59	Marian Hossa	21	Mike Sillinger	8	Mattias Ritola	1
Paul Coffey	49	Greg Johnson	21	Jason Woolley	8	Jiri Slegr	1
Jonathan Ericsson	49	Fredrik Olausson	21	Terry Carkner	7		
Dino Ciccarelli	47	Tomas Sandstrom	20	Dmitri Mironov	7		

TIMELINE

1997

Feb. 12 Collected three assists during Detroit's 7-1 win over the San Jose Sharks at Joe Louis Arena.

June 7 Scored the goal that gave Detroit the lead for good as the Wings won the Stanley Cup for the first time since 1955, sweeping the Philadelphia Flyers in the minimum four games via a 2-1 verdict in Game 4 at Joe Louis Arena.

Nov. 16 Scored twice on goalie Jeff Hackett as Detroit tied the Chicago Blackhawks 3-3 at the United Center.

Dec. 1 Selected to the Swedish team for the 1998 Nagano Winter Olympic Games.

Dec. 19 Scored twice on goalie Martin Brodeur in a 5-4 win over the New Jersey Devils at Joe Louis Arena.

Dec. 20 Voted the NHL's best defenseman in annual Toronto Sun poll of NHL players.

1998

Jan. 18 Played for the World Team in the NHL All-Star Game at Vancouver's GM Place.

Mar. 23 Scored once and assisted on three other goals as Detroit battled the Chicago Blackhawks to a 5-5 overtime tie at Joe Louis Arena.

Apr. 11 Collected two assists in a 5-2 win over the New York Rangers at Joe Louis Arena, finishing the season with 59 points to lead all NHL defensemen.

May 8 Collected three assists as Detroit won Game 6 of its opening-round Stanley Cup series over the Phoenix Coyotes 5-2 at America West Arena, clinching the series.

May 10 Nominated as a finalist for the Norris Trophy along with Chris Pronger of the St. Louis Blues and Rob Blake of the Los Angeles Kings.

May 19 Named to the NHL All-Star Team by The Sporting News.

May 29 Scored twice and assisted on another goal as Detroit downed the Dallas Stars 5-3 in Game 3 of the Western Conference finals at Joe Louis Arena.

June 9 Scored the game winner as Detroit beat the Washington Capitals 2-1 in Game 1 of the Stanley Cup finals at Joe Louis Arena. It was his sixth goal of the playoffs, tying the single-season Red Wings club record for a defenseman.

June 13 Assisted on a Steve Yzerman goal as Detroit beat the Washington Capitals 2-1 in Game 3 of the Stanley Cup finals at the MCI Center, establishing Detroit club records for assists (13) and points (19) by a defenseman in a single playoff year.

June 16 Won his second Stanley Cup as Detroit beat Washington 4-1 at the MCI Center to complete a sweep of the Capitals in the Cup finals.

June 25 Named to the NHL's First All-Star Team. Finished runner-up to Rob Blake of the Los Angeles Kings in voting for the Norris Trophy.

Aug. 1 Married his high-school sweetheart, Annika Eriksson, in Sweden.

Oct. 28 Scored a goal and added two assists in a 7-2 win over the Florida Panthers at the National Car Rental Center.

Nov. 10 Named along with Mats Sundin of the Toronto Maple Leafs as the best NHL player from Sweden in a poll of Swedish NHL players conducted by the Swedish news agency TT.

1999

Jan. 7 Voted a starter for the World Team in the Jan. 24 NHL All-Star Game at Tampa Bay's Ice Palace.

Jan. 16 Collected his 300th NHL assist on a goal by Igor Larionov in a 2-2 tie with the Vancouver Canucks at GM Place.

Jan. 24 Played in his third NHL All-Star Game for the World Team at Tampa Bay's

Nick's Sweden Teammates

PLAYER	GAMES	PLAYER	GAMES	PLAYER	GAMES	PLAYER	GAMES
Mats Sundin (F)	57	Andreas Johansson (F)	12	Niklas Brännström (F)	7	Magnus Arvedson (F)	4
Daniel Alfredsson (F)	30	Daniel Sedin (F)	12	Patric Englund (F)	7	Magnus Johansson (D)	4
Peter Forsberg (F	24	Henrik Sedin (F)	12	Patrik Ross (F)	7	Magnus Svensson (D)	4
Jonas Bergqvist (F)	23	Joakim Esbjörs (D)	12	Roger Johansson (D)	7	Marcus Nilson (F)	4
Jörgen Jönsson (F)	22	Niklas Sundström (F)	12	Tommy Söderström (GK)	7	Mathias Johansson (F)	4
Mattias Öhlund (D)	22	Thomas Forslund (F)	12	Anders Bröms (F)	6	Mats Lindgren (F)	4
Niklas Andersson (F)	22	Henrik Andersson (D)	11	Anders Carlsson (F)	6	Mattias Weinhandl (F)	4
Christian Bäckman (D)	20	Henrik Lundqvist (GK)	11	Börje Salming (D)	6	Mikel Tellqvist (GK)	4
Henrik Zetterberg (F)	20	Henrik Nilsson (F)	11	Dick Burlin (D)	6	Nicklas Bäckström (F)	4
Johan Garpenlöv (F)	20	Marcus Ragnarsson (D)	11	Johan Kejnemar (D)	6	Patric Hörnqvist (F)	4
Peter Andersson (D)	20	Bengt-Åke Gustafsson (F)	10	Lars Edström (F)	6	Patric Kjellberg (F)	4
Calle Johansson (D)	18	Fredrik Stillman (D)	10	Lars-Göran Wiklander (F)	6	Patrik Carnbäck (F)	4
Charles Berglund (F)	18	Håkan Loob (F)	10	Marcus Thuresson (F)	6	Roger Hansson (F)	4
Mikael Andersson (F)	18	Jan Viktorson (F)	10	Niklas Kronwall (D)	6	Stefan Örnskog (F)	4
P.J. Axelsson (F)	18	Kenneth Kennholt (D)	10	Osmo Soutokorva (D)	6	Tobias Enström (D)	4
Ulf Dahlén (F)	18	Patrik Juhlin (F)	10	Peter Eriksson (F)	6	Tommy Sjödin (D)	4
Samuel Påhlsson (F)	17	Per-Erik Eklund (F)	10	Stefan Elvenes (F)	6	Andreas Dackell (F)	3
Kjell Samuelsson (D)	16	Rolf Ridderwall (GK)	10	Thomas Steen (F)	6	Pelle Svensson (F)	3
Mats Näslund (F)	16	Tomas Jonsson (D)	10	Ulf Samuelsson (D)	6	Peter Popovic (D)	3
Mattias Norström (D)	16	Tomas Sandström (F)	10	Henrik Björkman (D)	5	Andreas Salomonsson (F)	2
Thomas Rundqvist (F)	16	Fredrik Nilsson (F)	9	Joakim Persson (GK)	5	Fredrik Sjöström (F)	2
Tomas Holmström (F)	16	Markus Näslund (F)	9	Patrik Högberg (F)	5	Jonas Höglund (F)	2
Fredrik Modin (F)	15	Niclas Hävelid (D)	9	Per Eklund (F)	5	Jonathan Hedström (F)	2
Kenny Jönsson (D)	15	Patrik Erickson (F)	9	Dick Tärnström (D)	4	Mathias Tjärnqvist (F)	2
Michael Nylander (F)	14	Ronnie Sundin (D)	9	Douglas Murray (D)	4	Per Hållberg (D)	2
Mikael Johansson (F)	14	Jonas Levén (GK)	8	Fredrik Olausson (D)	4	Johan Hedberg (GK)	1
Tommy Albelin (D)	14	Kim Johnsson (D)	8	Henrik Tallinder (D)	4	Jonas Gustavsson (GK)	1
Daniel Rydmark (F)	13	Mika Hannula (F)	8	Jan Larsson (F)	4	Leif Rohlin (D)	1
Daniel Tjärnqvist (D)	13	Mikael Renberg (F)	8	Johan Franzén (F)	4	Peter Lindmark (GK)	1
Tommy Salo (GK)	13	Mikael Samuelsson (F)	8	Johnny Oduya (D)	4	Roger Nordström (GK)	1
Torbjörn Lindberg (D)	13	Mattias Olsson (D)	7	Loui Eriksson (F)	4	Stefan Liv (GK)	1

TIMELINE

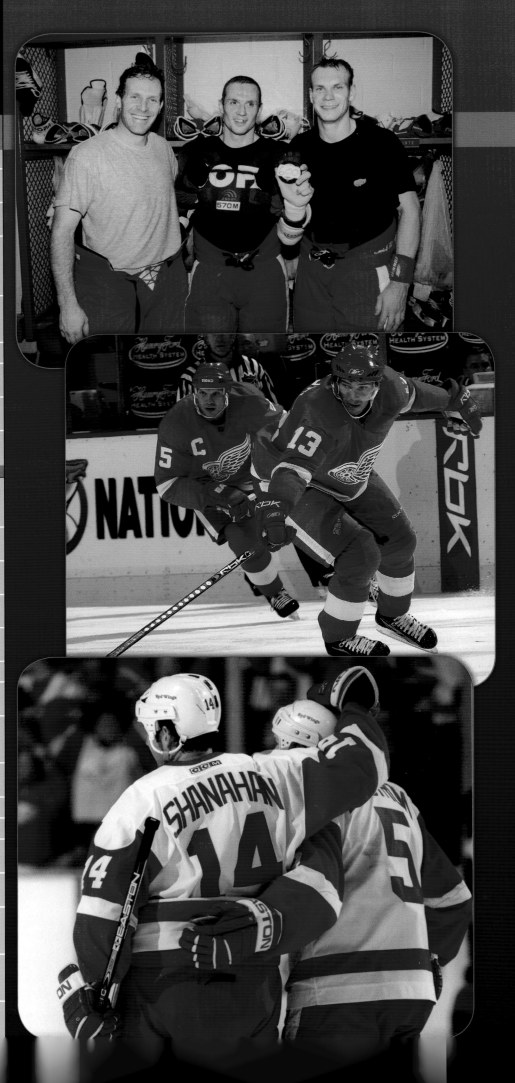

1999 continued

Mar. 19	Scored a shorthanded goal and set up two others as the Red Wings downed the Tampa Bay Lightning 5-3 at the Ice Palace.
Mar. 26	Scored his 100th NHL goal against Corey Schwab in Detroit's 6-1 win over the Tampa Bay Lightning at Joe Louis Arena.
May 4	Named a finalist for the Norris Trophy along with Ray Bourque of the Boston Bruins and Al MacInnis of the St. Louis Blues. Named a finalist for the Lady Byng Trophy along with Wayne Gretzky of the New York Rangers and Teemu Selanne of the Anaheim Mighty Ducks.
June 24	Finished as runner-up to Wayne Gretzky of the New York Rangers in Lady Byng Trophy voting. Finished as runner-up to Al MacInnis of the St. Louis Blues in Norris Trophy voting. Named to NHL First All-Star Team.
Aug. 20	Signed a three-year contract with the Red Wings.
Nov. 15	Scored once and set up two other goals as Detroit downed the Anaheim Mighty Ducks 6-3 at Joe Louis Arena.
Nov. 27	Drew the primary assist on Steve Yzerman's 600th NHL goal as Detroit downed the Edmonton Oilers 4-2.
Dec. 3	Scored a shorthanded goal, assisted on three other goals and was plus-five as the Wings defeated the Chicago Blackhawks 7-4 at the United Center.

2000

Jan. 8	Selected as a starter on the World Team for the Feb. 6 NHL All-Star Game at Toronto's Air Canada Centre. Led all defensemen in balloting with 924,024 votes.
Jan. 19	Logged 35:36 of ice time during a 3-3 overtime tie with the Vancouver Canucks at GM Place.
Jan. 22	Scored twice on goalie Ron Tugnutt as Detroit edged the Ottawa Senators 3-2 at the Corel Centre.
Feb. 4	Named captain of the World Team for the Feb. 6 NHL All-Star Game at Toronto's Air Canada Centre.
Feb. 6	Drew an assist for his first all-star game point as the World downed North America 9-4 in the NHL All-Star Game at Toronto's Air Canada Centre.
Mar.10-29	Enjoyed a career-high 10-game point-scoring streak.
Mar. 18	Collected three assists during a 4-3 win over the Colorado Avalanche at the Pepsi Center.
Apr. 2	Reached the 20-goal plateau for the first time with a tally against goalie Jeff Hackett as the Wings recorded a 6-5 overtime decision over the Montreal Canadiens at Joe Louis Arena.
Apr. 7	Finished the regular season with career highs in goals (20), assists (53) and points (73).
Apr. 18	Awarded the Viking Award as the top Swedish player in the NHL.
May 2	Announced as a finalist for both the Norris and Lady Byng Trophies.
June 15	Finished as runner-up in Norris and Lady Byng Trophy voting. Named to NHL First All-Star Team.
Sept. 12	Opened Bars And Stars, a restaurant in his hometown of Vasteras, Sweden, along with his partner, Edmonton Oilers goalie Tommy Salo.
Oct.	Collected his 500th NHL point, an assist on a Brendan Shanahan goal, during a 5-4 overtime victory against the Buffalo Sabres at Joe Louis Arena.
Oct. 28	Two assists in a 4-1 victory over the Columbus Blue Jackets gave Lidstrom 383 for his career, shattering Reed Larson's Red Wings mark for a defenseman.
Nov. 20	Scored twice, ending a 21-game goalless drought, and assisted on another goal as Detroit doubled the Nashville Predators 6-3 at Joe Louis Arena

Assists on Nick's Goals

PLAYER	ASSISTS	PLAYER	ASSISTS	PLAYER	ASSISTS	PLAYER	ASSISTS
Pavel Datsyuk	48	Martin Lapointe	8	Kirk Maltby	3	Shawn Burr	1
Steve Yzerman	42	Todd Bertuzzi	6	Mikael Samuelsson	3	Tim Cheveldae	1
Sergei Fedorov	33	Doug Brown	6	Boyd Devereaux	2	Steve Chiasson	1
Brendan Shanahan	26	Chris Chelios	6	Dallas Drake	2	Jonathan Ericsson	1
Henrik Zetterberg	25	Brett Hull	6	Steve Duchesne	2	Bob Errey	1
Igor Larionov	24	Dino Ciccarelli	5	Johan Franzen	2	Darren Helm	1
Vyacheslav Kozlov	17	Daniel Cleary	5	Marian Hossa	2	Jim Hiller	1
Tomas Holmstrom	16	Mathieu Dandenault	5	Vladimir Konstantinov	2	Mark Howe	1
Paul Coffey	14	Greg Johnson	5	Drew Miller	2	Brad McCrimmon	1
Larry Murphy	13	Niklas Kronwall	5	Brad Stuart	2	Kevin Miller	1
Brian Rafalski	13	Luc Robitaille	5	Tim Taylor	2	Mark Mowers	1
Kris Draper	10	Ray Sheppard	5	Ray Whitney	2	Fredrik Olausson	1
Robert Lang	10	Jiri Hudler	4	Jason Williams	2	Bob Probert	1
Darren McCarty	10	Keith Primeau	4	Sean Avery	1	Bob Rouse	1
Mathieu Schneider	10	Ian White	4	Marc Bergevin	1	Pat Verbeek	1
Valtteri Filppula	9	Jimmy Carson	3	Fabian Brunnstrom	1	Paul Yzeabaert	1

Nick's Regular-Season Assists

PLAYER	ASSISTS	PLAYER	ASSISTS	PLAYER	ASSISTS	PLAYER	ASSISTS
Tomas Holmstrom	76	Pat Verbeek	11	Greg Johnson	4	Jim Hiller	1
Steve Yzerman	76	Paul Ysebaert	11	Boyd Devereaux	3	Alan Kerr	1
Sergei Fedorov	75	Doug Brown	10	Patrick Eaves	3	Tomas Kopecky	1
Brendan Shanahan	73	Kirk Maltby	10	Darren Helm	3	Brett Lebda	1
Henrik Zetterberg	59	Brian Rafalski	10	Sheldon Kennedy	3	Ville Leino	1
Pavel Datsyuk	45	Jimmy Carson	9	Vladimir Konstantinov	3	Brad McCrimmon	1
Vyacheslav Kozlov	35	Paul Coffey	9	Bob Probert	3	Drew Miller	1
Johan Franzen	25	Luc Robitaille	9	Tim Taylor	3	Kevin Miller	1
Brett Hull	23	Shawn Burr	8	Jonathan Ericsson	2	Mike Modano	1
Daniel Cleary	22	Niklas Kronwall	8	Brent Gilchrist	2	Mark Mowers	1
Kris Draper	22	Robert Lang	8	Mike Krushelnyski	2	Brad Stuart	1
Darren McCarty	20	Jason Williams	8	Stacy Roest	2	Bob Rouse	1
Martin Lapointe	18	Todd Bertuzzi	7	Jason Abdelkader	1	Tomas Sandstrom	1
Dino Ciccarelli	16	Jiri Hudler	7	Sean Avery	1	Mike Sillinger	1
Igor Larionov	16	Marian Hossa	6	Chris Chelios	1	Steve Thomas	1
Ray Sheppard	16	Keith Primeau	5	Wendel Clark	1	Ray Whitney	1
Mikael Samuelsson	14	Steve Chiasson	4	Steve Duchesne	1	Ian White	1
Valtteri Filppula	13	Mathieu Dandenault	4	Bob Errey	1	Jason York	1
Larry Murphy	12	Dallas Drake	4	Brent Fedyk	1		
Mathieu Schneider	11	Gerard Gallant	4	Todd Gill	1		

TIMELINE

Jan. 4 — Collected three assists as Detroit downed the Dallas Stars 4-2 at Joe Louis Arena.

Jan. 13 — Voted to the World Team starting lineup for the Feb. 4 NHL All-Star Game at Colorado's Pepsi Center.

Feb. 4 — Scored a goal as the World beat North America 14-12 in the NHL All-Star Game at Colorado's Pepsi Center.

Feb. 23 — Garnered a trio of assists as the Red Wings defeated the St. Louis Blues 4-2 at Joe Louis Arena.

Feb. 25 — Collected three assists for the second straight game as Detroit beat the Phoenix Coyotes 6-3 at Joe Louis Arena.

Mar. 15 — Scored once and set up two other goals as Detroit dropped the Calgary Flames 5-2 at Joe Louis Arena.

Mar. 21 — Named to the Swedish team for the 2002 Winter Olympic Games in Salt Lake City.

Mar. 31 — Took stitches to the nose and face after being cut by the skate of Philadelphia forward Paul Ranheim during a 1-0 win over the Flyers at the First Union Center.

Apr. 5 — Produced his fourth three-assist game of the season as Detroit shutout the Atlanta Thrashers 4-0 at Joe Louis Arena.

Apr. 7 — An assist on a Slava Kozlov goal in a 4-3 win over the Colorado Avalanche at Joe Louis Arena gave Lidstrom a career-high 56 assists on the season.

Apr. 23 — Collecting a point in all six games, Lidstrom finished as Detroit's playoff scoring leader with a goal and seven assists.

May 11 — Named a finalist for both the Norris and Lady Byng Trophies.

May 21 — Named to the NHL All-Star Team selected by The Sporting News.

June 14 — Won his first Norris Trophy as the NHL's best defenseman, the first European-born and trained player to win the award. Finished runner-up in Lady Byng Trophy voting. Named to NHL First All-Star Team.

Aug. 22 — Attended Swedish Olympic training camp in Sigtuna, Sweden.

Oct. 12 — An assist on a Brendan Shanahan goal during a 4-2 win over the Buffalo Sabres at Joe Louis Arena is Lidstrom's 571st point as a Red Wing, surpassing Reed Larson's club record for defensemen.

Oct. 24 — Collected three assists during a 4-1 victory over the Edmonton Oilers at Joe Louis Arena.

Dec. 6 — Signed a two-year contract extension with Detroit.

Jan. 6 — Named the NHL's best defenseman in annual Toronto Sun poll of NHL players.

Jan. 12 — Voted a starter on the World Team for the Feb. 2 NHL All-Star Game at Staples Center in Los Angeles. Lidstrom led all players, garnering 211,486 votes.

Jan. 25 — An assist on an Igor Larionov goal during a 4-1 win over the Phoenix Coyotes is Lidstrom's 600th NHL point.

Feb. 2 — Helped the World to an 8-5 win over North America in the NHL All-Star Game at Staples Center in Los Angeles.

Feb. 15-21 — Played for Sweden in Winter Olympic Games at Salt Lake City, collecting a goal and five assists in four games.

Mar. 13 — Scored twice on goalie Jussi Markkanen as Detroit edged the Edmonton Oilers 4-3 in overtime at Joe Louis Arena.

Mar. 21 — Assisted on all three goals during a 3-2 overtime decision at Nationwide Arena against the Columbus Blue Jackets.

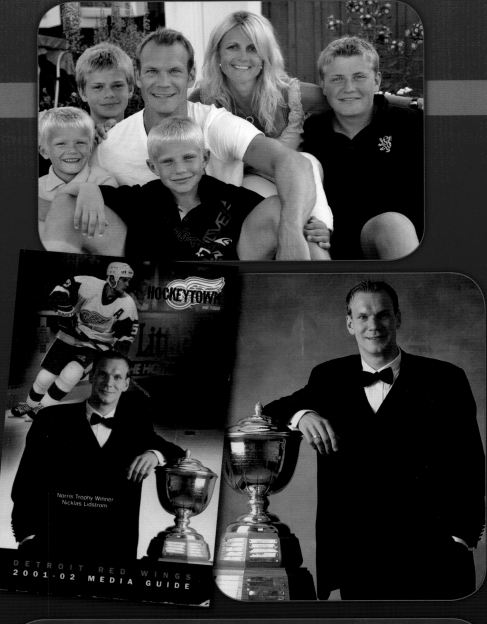

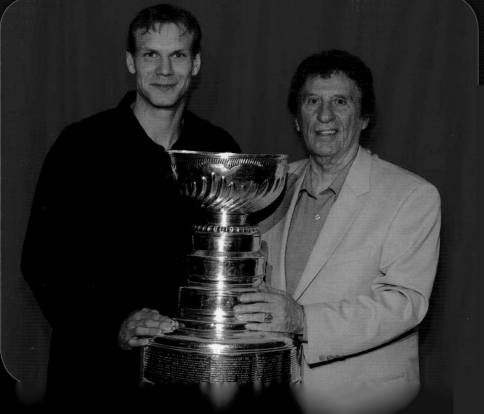

Teammates' Assists on Lidstrom Power-Play Goals

REGULAR SEASON

PLAYER	TOTAL	PLAYER	TOTAL
Pavel Datsyuk	27	Steve Duchesne	2
Steve Yzerman	22	Jiri Hudler	2
Sergei Fedorov	19	Vladimir Konstantinov	2
Brendan Shanahan	17	Keith Primeau	2
Igor Larionov	17	Luc Robitaille	2
Tomas Holmstrom	13	Ian White	2
Paul Coffey	12	Sean Avery	1
Henrik Zetterberg	12	Doug Brown	1
Brian Rafalski	11	Chris Chelios	1
Vyacheslav Kozlov	8	Tim Cheveldae	1
Robert Lang	8	Steve Chiasson	1
Mathieu Schneider	8	Dallas Drake	1
Larry Murphy	5	Johan Franzen	1
Valtteri Filppula	4	Marian Hossa	1
Brett Hull	4	Kirk Maltby	1
Martin Lapointe	4	Brad McCrimmon	1
Darren McCarty	4	Drew Miller	1
Ray Sheppard	4	Kevin Miller	1
Dino Ciccarelli	3	Mike Modano	1
Daniel Cleary	3	Fredrik Olausson	1
Greg Johnson	3	Bob Probert	1
Niklas Kronwall	3	Tim Taylor	1
Mikael Samuelsson	3	Pat Verbeek	1
Todd Bertuzzi	2	Jason Williams	1
Jimmy Carson	2		

PLAYOFFS

PLAYER	TOTAL	PLAYER	TOTAL
Tomas Holmstrom	52	Marian Hossa	3
Brendan Shanahan	49	Jiri Hudler	3
Steve Yzerman	46	Paul Ysebaert	3
Sergei Fedorov	33	Todd Bertuzzi	2
Henrik Zetterberg	28	Doug Brown	2
Pavel Datsyuk	26	Valtteri Filppula	2
Johan Franzen	18	Gerard Gallant	2
Vyacheslav Kozlov	16	Brent Gilchrist	2
Brett Hull	15	Bob Probert	2
Dino Ciccarelli	12	Shawn Burr	1
Igor Larionov	11	Chris Chelios	1
Mathieu Schneider	11	Steve Chiasson	1
Ray Sheppard	11	Mathieu Dandenault	1
Martin Lapointe	10	Dallas Drake	1
Brian Rafalski	10	Kris Draper	1
Daniel Cleary	9	Steve Duchesne	1
Larry Murphy	9	Jonathan Ericsson	1
Robert Lang	8	Greg Johnson	1
Niklas Kronwall	7	Vladimir Konstantinov	1
Pat Verbeek	7	Tomas Kopecky	1
Jimmy Carson	6	Brett Lebda	1
Darren McCarty	6	Kevin Miller	1
Luc Robitaille	6	Mike Modano	1
Mikael Samuelsson	5	Stacy Roest	1
Jason Williams	5	Ray Whitney	1
Paul Coffey	4		

Lidstrom Assists on Teammates' Power-Play Goals

REGULAR SEASON

PLAYER	TOTAL	PLAYER	TOTAL
Steve Yzerman	8	Brendan Shanahan	2
Daniel Cleary	3	Henrik Zetterberg	2
Paul Coffey	3	Todd Bertuzzi	1
Sergei Fedorov	3	Tim Cheveldae	1
Robert Lang	3	Steve Chiasson	1
Brian Rafalski	3	Dino Ciccarelli	1
Pavel Datsyuk	2	Marian Hossa	1
Valtteri Filppula	2	Brett Hull	1
Johan Franzen	2	Vyacheslav Kozlov	1
Tomas Holmstrom	2	Igor Larionov	1
Larry Murphy	2	Mikael Samuelsson	1
Mathieu Schneider	2	Brad Stuart	1

PLAYOFFS

PLAYER	TOTAL	PLAYER	TOTAL
Tomas Holmstrom	11	Brendan Shanahan	2
Pavel Datsyuk	7	Pat Verbeek	2
Sergei Fedorov	7	Doug Brown	1
Steve Yzerman	7	Wendel Clark	1
Henrik Zetterberg	5	Steve Duchesne	1
Johan Franzen	4	Greg Johnson	1
Vyacheslav Kozlov	4	Martin Lapointe	1
Brian Rafalski	4	Fredrik Olausson	1
Paul Coffey	2	Keith Primeau	1
Marian Hossa	2	Mathieu Schneider	1
Brett Hull	2	Ray Sheppard	1
Igor Larionov	2	Brad Stuart	1

TIMELINE

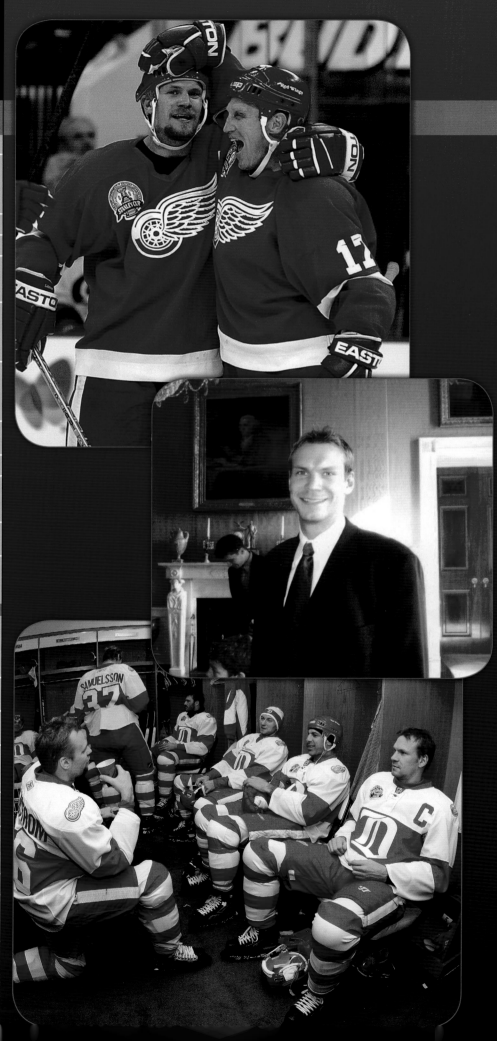

2002 continued

Apr. 10 — An assist in a 3-3 overtime tie with the Chicago Blackhawks at Joe Louis Arena gave Lidstrom 59 points for the season and a share of the NHL lead among defensemen with Sergei Gonchar of the Washington Capitals.

May 1 — Named a finalist for the Norris and Lady Byng Trophies.

May 14 — Named to the NHL All-Star Team announced by The Sporting News.

June 6 — Broke a 1-1 tie with a third-period power-play goal and then set up Kris Draper's insurance marker as Detroit downed the Carolina Hurricanes 3-1 at Joe Louis Arena to knot the Stanley Cup finals at one game apiece.

June 8 — Saw 52:03 of ice time in Detroit's 3-2 triple-overtime victory over the Carolina Hurricanes in Game 3 of the Stanley Cup finals. Brett Hull tipped home Lidstrom's point shot for the game-tying goal with 1:14 left in regulation time.

June 13 — Won his third Stanley Cup as Detroit downed the Carolina Hurricanes 3-1 in Game 5 of the Cup finals series at Joe Louis Arena. Awarded the Conn Smythe Trophy as Stanley Cup MVP, the first European-born and trained player to win the award.

June 20 — Won his second Norris Trophy as the NHL's best defenseman. Named to NHL First All-Star Team. Finished third in Lady Byng Trophy balloting.

Aug. 27 — Named the best player in the NHL by the Hockey News.

Nov. 7 — Scored to tie the game in the third period, and then set up Sergei Fedorov's game winner as Detroit took a 2-1 overtime decision from the Boston Bruins at Joe Louis Arena.

Dec. 21 — Figured in all three goals, scoring once and assisting on the other two, during a 3-2 victory over the New York Rangers at Joe Louis Arena.

Dec. 28 — An assist on a Sergei Fedorov goal during a 4-2 win over the Nashville Predators at the Gaylord Entertainment Center is Lidstrom's 500th NHL assist.

2003

Jan. 10 — Voted a starter for the Feb. 2 NHL All-Star Game at Minnesota's Xcel Energy Center, leading fan balloting for the second straight year, garnering 164,568 votes. It's Lidstrom's fifth straight year as a starter in the game.

Jan. 13 — Scored two goals, including the game-winner 47 seconds into overtime, as Detroit downed the Chicago Blackhawks 5-4 at Joe Louis Arena.

Jan. 19 — Collected an assist on a Tomas Holmstrom goal during his 900th NHL game, a 4-1 loss to the Vancouver Canucks at Joe Louis Arena.

Feb. 2 — Played in his seventh NHL All-Star Game, collecting an assist as the Western Conference downed the Eastern Conference 6-5 in a shootout at Florida's Office Depot Center.

Mar. 7 — Matched a career-high with four assists during a 7-2 rout of the St. Louis Blues at Joe Louis Arena.

Mar. 29 — Beat Chris Osgood for his 18th goal of the season during a 6-2 win over the St. Louis Blues at the Savvis Center, giving Lidstrom the lead among NHL defensemen.

Apr. 29 — Named a finalist for the Norris and Lady Byng Trophies.

June 11 — Became the first defenseman since Bobby Orr to win three consecutive Norris Trophies. Named to NHL First All-Star Team and finished runner-up in Lady Byng Trophy voting.

June 29 — Named the top NHL defenseman by the Hockey News.

Oct. 11 — Scored on goalie Patrick Lalime 2:08 into overtime to give Detroit a 3-2 decision over the Ottawa Senators at the Corel Centre.

Nov. 4 — Voted the fourth greatest Swedish hockey player of all-time in a poll conducted by Swedish newspaper Dagens Nyheter.

Playoff Assists on Lidstrom Goals

PLAYER	ASSISTS	PLAYER	ASSISTS	PLAYER	ASSISTS	PLAYER	ASSISTS
Steve Yzerman	13	Todd Bertuzzi	1	Niklas Kronwall	5	Fabian Brunnstrom	1
Pavel Datsyuk	7	Tim Cheveldae	1	Luc Robitaille	5	Shawn Burr	1
Sergei Fedorov	5	Steve Chiasson	1	Ray Sheppard	5	Tim Cheveldae	1
Vyacheslav Kozlov	5	Dino Ciccarelli	1	Jiri Hudler	4	Steve Chiasson	1
Brian Rafalski	5	Viacheslav Fetisov	1	Keith Primeau	4	Jonathan Ericsson	1
Henrik Zetterberg	5	Marian Hossa	1	Ian White	4	Bob Errey	1
Paul Coffey	4	Jiri Hudler	1	Jimmy Carson	3	Darren Helm	1
Tomas Holmstrom	4	Brett Hull	1	Kirk Maltby	3	Jim Hiller	1
Robert Lang	4	Martin Lapointe	1	Mikael Samuelsson	3	Mark Howe	1
Daniel Cleary	4	Kirk Maltby	1	Boyd Devereaux	2	Brad McCrimmon	1
Kris Draper	3	Keith Primeau	1	Dallas Drake	2	Kevin Miller	1
Larry Murphy	3	Mikael Samuelsson	1	Steve Duchesne	2	Mark Mowers	1
Mathieu Schneider	3	Brad Stuart	1	Vladimir Konstantinov	2	Fredrik Olausson	1
Chris Chelios	2	Martin Lapointe	8	Drew Miller	2	Bob Probert	1
Valtteri Filppula	2	Doug Brown	6	Tim Taylor	2	Bob Rouse	1
Johan Franzen	2	Brett Hull	6	Ray Whitney	2	Pat Verbeek	1
Igor Larionov	2	Dino Ciccarelli	5	Jason Williams	2	Paul Yzeabaert	1
Darren McCarty	2	Mathieu Dandenault	5	Sean Avery	1		
Brendan Shanahan	2	Greg Johnson	5	Marc Bergevin	1		

Nick's Playoff Assists

PLAYER	ASSISTS	PLAYER	ASSISTS	PLAYER	ASSISTS	PLAYER	ASSISTS
Tomas Holmstrom	14	Kris Draper	4	Darren McCarty	2	Brent Gilchrist	1
Steve Yzerman	13	Igor Larionov	4	Mathieu Schneider	2	Darren Helm	1
Sergei Fedorov	12	Brian Rafalski	4	Pat Verbeek	2	Martin Lapointe	1
Pavel Datsyuk	10	Brett Hull	3	Doug Brown	1	Kirk Maltby	1
Henrik Zetterberg	10	Valtteri Filppula	2	Wendel Clark	1	Fredrik Olausson	1
Dino Ciccarelli	8	Chris Chelios	2	Daniel Cleary	1	Keith Primeau	1
Johan Franzen	6	Paul Coffey	2	Boyd Devereaux	1	Luc Robitaille	1
Vyacheslav Kozlov	5	Marian Hossa	2	Steve Duchesne	1	Ray Sheppard	1
Brendan Shanahan	5	Greg Johnson	2	Jonathan Ericsson	1	Brad Stuart	1

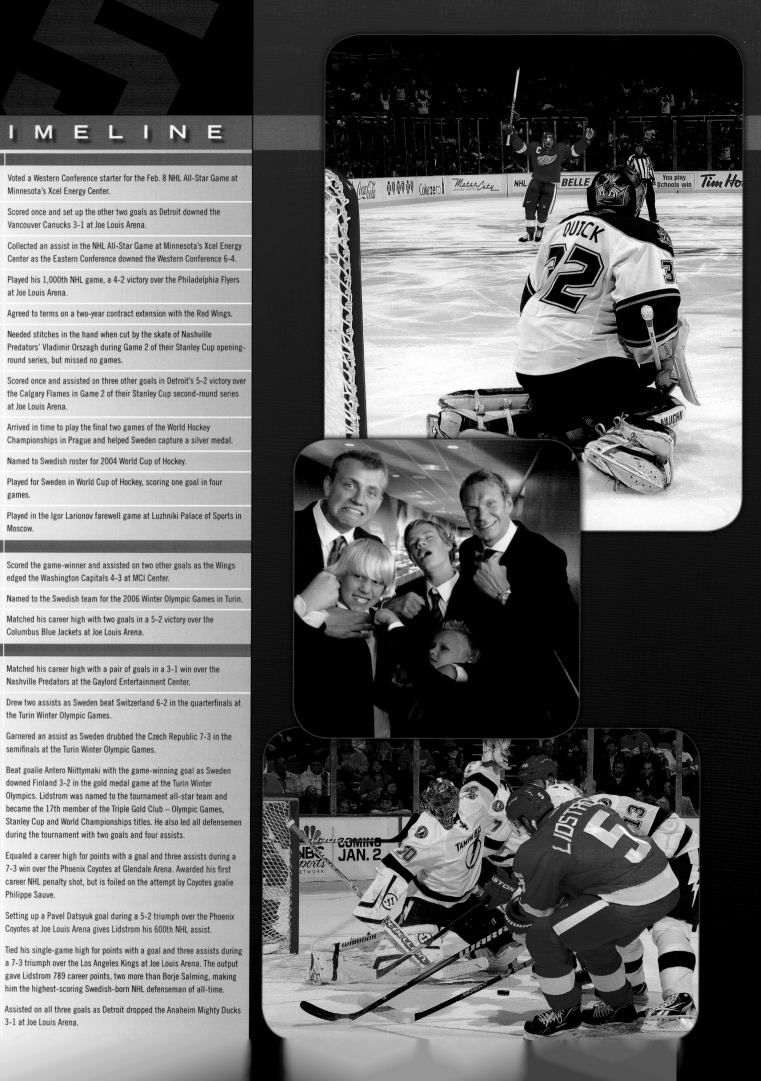

TIMELINE

2004

Jan. 8 — Voted a Western Conference starter for the Feb. 8 NHL All-Star Game at Minnesota's Xcel Energy Center.

Feb. 5 — Scored once and set up the other two goals as Detroit downed the Vancouver Canucks 3-1 at Joe Louis Arena.

Feb. 8 — Collected an assist in the NHL All-Star Game at Minnesota's Xcel Energy Center as the Eastern Conference downed the Western Conference 6-4.

Feb. 29 — Played his 1,000th NHL game, a 4-2 victory over the Philadelphia Flyers at Joe Louis Arena.

Apr. 2 — Agreed to terms on a two-year contract extension with the Red Wings.

Apr. 9 — Needed stitches in the hand when cut by the skate of Nashville Predators' Vladimir Orszagh during Game 2 of their Stanley Cup opening-round series, but missed no games.

Apr. 24 — Scored once and assisted on three other goals in Detroit's 5-2 victory over the Calgary Flames in Game 2 of their Stanley Cup second-round series at Joe Louis Arena.

May 4 — Arrived in time to play the final two games of the World Hockey Championships in Prague and helped Sweden capture a silver medal.

May 17 — Named to Swedish roster for 2004 World Cup of Hockey.

Aug. 31-Sept. 9 — Played for Sweden in World Cup of Hockey, scoring one goal in four games.

Dec. 13 — Played in the Igor Larionov farewell game at Luzhniki Palace of Sports in Moscow.

2005

Dec. 9 — Scored the game-winner and assisted on two other goals as the Wings edged the Washington Capitals 4-3 at MCI Center.

Dec. 22 — Named to the Swedish team for the 2006 Winter Olympic Games in Turin.

Dec. 31 — Matched his career high with two goals in a 5-2 victory over the Columbus Blue Jackets at Joe Louis Arena.

2006

Jan. 6 — Matched his career high with a pair of goals in a 3-1 win over the Nashville Predators at the Gaylord Entertainment Center.

Feb. 21 — Drew two assists as Sweden beat Switzerland 6-2 in the quarterfinals at the Turin Winter Olympic Games.

Feb. 23 — Garnered an assist as Sweden drubbed the Czech Republic 7-3 in the semifinals at the Turin Winter Olympic Games.

Feb. 26 — Beat goalie Antero Niittymaki with the game-winning goal as Sweden downed Finland 3-2 in the gold medal game at the Turin Winter Olympics. Lidstrom was named to the tournament all-star team and became the 17th member of the Triple Gold Club – Olympic Games, Stanley Cup and World Championships titles. He also led all defensemen during the tournament with two goals and four assists.

Mar. 4 — Equaled a career high for points with a goal and three assists during a 7-3 win over the Phoenix Coyotes at Glendale Arena. Awarded his first career NHL penalty shot, but is foiled on the attempt by Coyotes goalie Philippe Sauve.

Mar. 7 — Setting up a Pavel Datsyuk goal during a 5-2 triumph over the Phoenix Coyotes at Joe Louis Arena gives Lidstrom his 600th NHL assist.

Mar. 13 — Tied his single-game high for points with a goal and three assists during a 7-3 triumph over the Los Angeles Kings at Joe Louis Arena. The output gave Lidstrom 789 career points, two more than Borje Salming, making him the highest-scoring Swedish-born NHL defenseman of all-time.

Mar. 15 — Assisted on all three goals as Detroit dropped the Anaheim Mighty Ducks 3-1 at Joe Louis Arena.

Regular-Season Goaltenders Scored On

PLAYER	GOALS	PLAYER	GOALS	PLAYER	GOALS	PLAYER	GOALS
Ed Belfour	11	Steve Mason	3	Patrick Lalime	2	Jeff Harding	1
Nikolai Khabibulin	11	Andy Moog	3	Michael Leighton	2	Brian Hayward	1
Ilya Bryzgalov	7	Steve Passmore	3	Jussi Markkanen	2	Ron Hextall	1
Tomas Vokoun	7	Bill Ranford	3	Ryan Miller	2	Milan Hlinicka	1
Jeff Hackett	6	Pekka Rinne	3	Fredrik Norrena	2	Olaf Kolzig	1
Guy Hebert	6	Mikhail Shtalenkov	3	Chris Osgood	2	Blaine Lacher	1
Felix Potvin	6	Chris Terreri	3	Mike Richter	2	Pascal Leclaire	1
Empty Net	6	Marty Turco	3	Curtis Sanford	2	Kari Lehtonen	1
Miikka Kiprusoff	5	Roman Turek	3	Corey Schwab	2	Darrin Madeley	1
Patrick Roy	5	Darcy Wakaluk	3	Jamie Storr	2	Curtis McElhinney	1
Sean Burke	4	Jean-Sebastien Aubin	2	Rick Tabaracci	2	Evgeni Nabokov	1
Marc Denis	4	Alex Auld	2	John Tanner	2	Antti Niemi	1
Arturs Irbe	4	Jason Bacashihua	2	Jocelyn Thibault	2	Carey Price	1
Curtis Joseph	4	Brian Boucher	2	Mike Vernon	2	Daren Puppa	1
Manny Legace	4	Fred Brathwaite	2	Cam Ward	2	Jonathan Quick	1
Kirk McLean	4	Byron Dafoe	2	Niklas Backstrom	1	Vincent Riendeau	1
Dwayne Roloson	4	Manny Fernandez	2	Don Beaupre	1	Dominic Roussel	1
Tommy Salo	4	Mark Fitzpatrick	2	John Blue	1	Tommy Soderstrom	1
Ron Tugnutt	4	Grant Fuhr	2	Peter Budaj	1	Robb Stauber	1
Martin Brodeur	3	Jean-Sebastien Giguere	2	Jon Casey	1	Jose Theodore	1
Dan Cloutier	3	John Grahame	2	Corey Crawford	1	Tim Thomas	1
Mike Dunham	3	Glenn Healy	2	Jeff Drouin-Deslauriers	1	Vesa Toskala	1
Dan Ellis	3	Jonas Hiller	2	Devan Dubnyk	1	Semyon Varlamov	1
Jaroslav Halak	3	Corey Hirsch	2	Brian Elliott	1	John Vanbiesbrouck	1
Trevor Kidd	3	Cristobal Huet	2	Stephane Fiset	1	Derek Wilkinson	1
Roberto Luongo	3	Pat Jablonski	2	Wade Flaherty	1	Ken Wregget	1
Chris Mason	3	Jason Labarbera	2	Marc-Andre Fleury	1		

Playoff Goaltenders Scored On

PLAYER	GOALS	PLAYER	GOALS	PLAYER	GOALS	PLAYER	GOALS
Patrick Roy	5	Miikka Kiprusoff	3	Grant Fuhr	1	Peter Skudra	1
Jon Casey	4	Andy Moog	3	Jean-Sebastien Giguere	1	Jamie Storr	1
Arturs Irbe	4	Dan Cloutier	2	Ron Hextall	1	Tomas Vokoun	1
Antti Niemi	4	Dan Ellis	2	Olaf Kolzig	1	Empty Net	1
Ed Belfour	3	Jonas Hiller	2	Steve Mason	1		
Ilya Bryzgalov	3	Evgeni Nabokov	2	Dwayne Roloson	1		
Nikolai Khabibulin	3	Felix Potvin	2	Mikhail Shtalenkov	1		

TIMELINE

2006 continued

Apr. 13	Scored once and assisted on three other goals in a 7-3 win over the Chicago Blackhawks at the United Center. Lidstrom's 64 assists are a new Detroit single-season club record for a defenseman.
Apr. 15	Scored a goal in a 3-2 win over the St. Louis Blues at the Savvis Center, finishing the season with 80 points, a new Detroit single-season club record for a defenseman. It was also his 189th career NHL goal, surpassing Reed Larson's career mark for a Red Wings' defenseman.
Apr. 18	Won the Viking Award as the top Swedish player in the NHL.
May 4	Named a finalist for the Norris Trophy.
June 21	Won his fourth Norris Trophy as the NHL's best defenseman. Named to NHL First All-Star Team.
June 29	Agreed to terms on a two-year deal with the Red Wings.
Oct. 5	Named captain of the Red Wings.
Oct. 11	Recorded three assists as the Wings routed the Phoenix Coyotes 9-2 at Joe Louis Arena.
Oct. 27	Scored two goals in a 4-3 win over the Dallas Stars at American Airlines Center.
Nov. 23	Served as grand marshal for America's Thanksgiving Parade in Detroit.
Dec. 10	Named the best European-trained player in NHL history by the Hockey News.

2007

Jan. 9	Voted to Western Conference starting lineup for the Jan. 24 NHL All-Star Game at American Airlines Center in Dallas.
Jan. 24	Drew an assist as the West downed the East 12-9 in the NHL All-Star Game at American Airlines Center in Dallas.
Jan. 30	Assisted on all four goals as Detroit posted a 4-3 overtime victory over the New York Islanders at Nassau Veterans Memorial Coliseum.
Feb. 2	Collected three assists, giving him eight assists in the last three games, as Detroit downed the St. Louis Blues 5-3 at Joe Louis Arena.
Feb. 11	Canadian-based TSN named Lidstrom the best Swedish player in NHL history.
Mar. 2	Beat goalie Nikolai Khabibulin in a 6-2 win over the Chicago Blackhawks at Joe Louis for his 200th NHL goal and 100th NHL power-play goal. Also had two assists.
Apr. 1-5	Missed two games due to back spasms.
Apr. 21	Collected four assists during a 5-1 victory over the Calgary Flames in Game 5 of their Stanley Cup Western Conference quarterfinals to tie the Red Wings playoff record for assists in a playoff game.
Apr. 30	Named a finalist for the Norris Trophy.
May 22	An assist on a Pavel Datsyuk goal in Game 6 of their Western Conference finals series with the Anaheim Ducks at the Honda Center was Lidstrom's 18th point, which led the Red Wings and all NHL defensemen in playoff scoring.
June 13	Won Norris Trophy as NHL's best defenseman for the fifth time. Named to NHL First All-Star Team.
Oct. 8	Two assists in a 4-2 victory over the Edmonton Oilers at Joe Louis Arena gave Lidstrom 873 points, moving him past Peter Forsberg and into second place in career scoring among the NHL's Swedish-born players.
Nov. 18	Scored once and assisted on two other goals in Detroit's 5-4 shootout victory over the Columbus Blue Jackets at Nationwide Arena.
Nov. 27	Playing his 1,200th NHL game, Lidstrom collects two assists in a 5-3 victory over the Calgary Flames at Joe Louis Arena. Lidstrom became just the 12th NHL player to play 1,200 games for one NHL team.

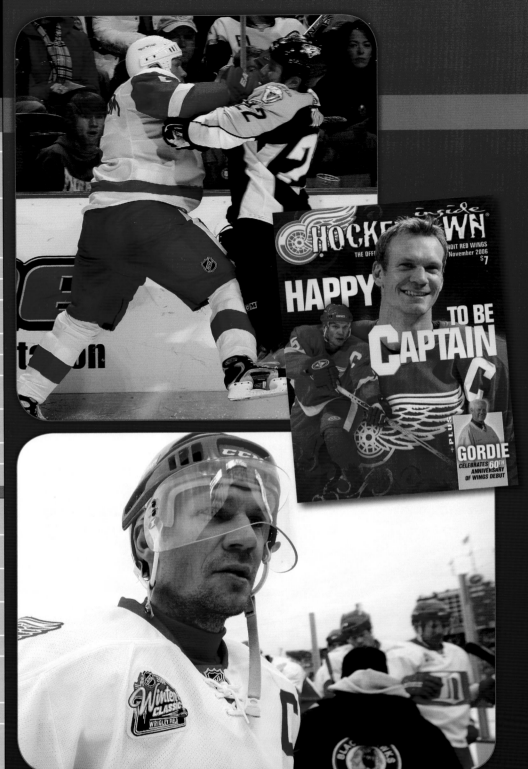

*-Also known as Arrowhead Pond (1993-94 to 2005-06).
@-Also known as Fleet Center (1995-96 to 2003-04).
$-Also known as Marine Midland Center (1996-97 to 1998-99) and HSBC Arena (1999-2000 to 2010-11).
#-Also known as Canadian Airlines Saddledome (1995-96 to 2000-01) and Olympic Saddledome (1991-92 to 1994-95).
%-Also known as Raleigh Entertainment and Sports Arena (1999-2000 to 2001-02).
^-Also known as Northlands Coliseum (1991-92 to 1994-95), Edmonton Coliseum (1995-96 to 1998-99) and SkyReach Centre (1999-2000 to 2002-03).
&-Also known as National Car Rental Center (1998-99 to 2001-02) and Office Depot Center (2002-03 to 2003-04).
+-Also known as Molson Centre (1995-96 to 2002-03).
<-Also known as Nashville Arena (1998-99; 2005-06 to 2006-07; 2009-10), Gaylord Entertainment Center (1999-2000 to 2004-05) and Sommet Center (2007-08 to 2009-10).
>-Also known as Byrne Meadowlands Arena (1991-92) and Meadowlands Arena (1992-93 to 1995-96)
~-Also known as The Spectrum (1991-92 to 1994-95).
x-Also known as the Palladium (1995-96), Corel Centre (1995-96 to 2005-06).
y-Also known as Glendale Arena (2003-04 to 2006-07).
**-Also known as First Union Center (1998-99 to 2002-03).
***-Also known as Civic Arena (1991-92 to 1999-2000).
****-Also known as Kiel Center (1994-95 to 1999-2000) and Savvis Center (2000-01 to 2006-07).
z-Also known as San Jose Arena (1993-94 to 2000-01) and Compaq Center (2001-02).
1-Also known as Ice Palace (1996-97 to 2001-02).
2-Also known as GM Place (1995-96 to 2009-10).
3-Also known as Capital Centre (1991-92 to 1992-93).
4-Also known as MCI Center (1997-98 to 2005-06).
5-Site of neutral-site games played in 1992-93 (vs. Philadelphia) and 1993-94 (vs. Hartford).
6-Site of neutral-site game played in 1992-93 vs. Washington.
7-Site of neutral-site game played in 1993-94 vs. Tampa Bay.

Regular-Season Arenas Played In

Arena (Team)	GP	G	A	PTS	PIM
Honda Center (Anaheim)*	34	5	16	21	14
Philips Arena (Atlanta)	6	1	6	7	0
Boston Garden (Boston)	3	1	1	2	0
TD Banknorth Garden (Boston)@	12	3	6	9	2
Memorial Auditorium (Buffalo)	4	0	2	2	0
First Niagara Center (Buffalo) $	10	2	4	6	0
Pengrowth Saddledome (Calgary)#	39	2	19	21	8
Greensboro Coliseum (Carolina)	2	0	0	0	0
RBC Center (Carolina)%	7	1	5	6	2
Chicago Stadium (Chicago)	11	3	2	5	4
United Center (Chicago)	48	13	28	41	6
McNichols Arena (Colorado)	8	2	5	7	2
Pepsi Center (Colorado)	23	5	20	25	8
Nationwide Arena (Columbus)	32	4	14	18	22
Reunion Arena (Dallas)	15	3	5	8	6
American Airlines Arena (Dallas)	22	4	10	14	6
Joe Louis Arena (Detroit)	790	147	488	635	264
Rexall Place (Edmonton)^	38	5	22	27	18
Miami Arena (Florida)	4	0	1	1	0
Bank Atlantic Center (Florida)&	8	2	5	7	0
Hartford Civic Center (Hartford)	5	0	0	0	4
Great Western Forum (Los Angeles)	16	0	7	7	10
STAPLES Center (Los Angeles)	22	5	10	15	2
Metropolitan Sports Center (Minnesota)	8	1	3	4	4
Xcel Energy Center (Minnesota)	22	4	11	15	4
Montreal Forum (Montreal)	4	0	1	1	0
Bell Centre (Montreal)+	9	1	4	5	4
Bridgestone Arena (Nashville)<	38	5	12	17	12
Continental Airlines Arena (New Jersey)>	12	0	10	10	0
Prudential Center (New Jersey)	2	0	0	0	0
Nassau Veterans' Memorial Coliseum (NY Islanders)	15	2	9	11	4
Madison Square Garden (New York Rangers)	13	4	8	12	0
Ottawa Civic Centre (Ottawa)	2	0	0	0	0
Scotiabank Place (Ottawa)-x	10	3	5	8	2
CoreStates Spectrum (Philadelphia)~	6	0	1	1	2
Wachovia Center (Philadelphia)**	5	0	0	0	2
America West Arena (Phoenix)	18	2	7	9	8
Jobing.com Arena (Phoenix)-y	14	3	14	17	6
Mellon Arena (Pittsburgh)***	14	1	7	8	4
Consol Energy Center (Pittsburgh)	2	0	0	0	0
Colisee (Quebec)	4	2	2	4	0
St. Louis Arena (St. Louis)	11	0	8	8	6
Scottrade Center (St. Louis)****	50	8	13	21	16
Cow Palace (San Jose)	4	1	1	2	2
HP Pavilion (San Jose)-z	33	7	21	28	16
Expo Hall (Tampa Bay)	4	0	4	4	0
Thunderdome (Tampa Bay)	2	0	2	2	0
St. Pete Times Forum (Tampa Bay)-1	10	1	11	12	4
Maple Leaf Gardens (Toronto)	20	3	17	20	6
Air Canada Centre (Toronto)	7	1	3	4	2
Pacific Coliseum (Vancouver)	6	0	3	3	0
Rogers Arena (Vancouver)-2	31	4	10	14	10
US Air Arena (Washington)-3	5	0	4	4	12
Verizon Center (Washington)-4	10	1	7	8	6
Winnipeg Arena (Winnipeg)	10	1	2	3	2
Richfield Coliseum-5	2	1	0	1	0
Bradley Center-6	1	0	0	0	0
Target Center-7	1	0	2	2	0
Wrigley Field	1	0	0	0	0
TOTALS	1564	264	878	1142	514

TIMELINE

2008

Jan. 2 An assist on a Pavel Datsyuk goal during a 4-1 win over the Dallas Stars at Joe Louis Arena is the 700th of Lidstrom's NHL career.

Jan. 8 Named a starter for the Jan. 27 NHL All-Star Game at Philips Arena in Atlanta. Lidstrom led all Western Conference vote-getters with 477,787.

Jan. 19 Scored once and set up two other goals as Detroit doubled the San Jose Sharks 6-3 at HP Pavilion.

Jan. 27 Played in his 10th NHL All-Star Game as the East edged the West 8-7 at Philips Arena in Atlanta.

Jan. 30 Tallied the winning goal and assisted on two others as the Wings edged the Phoenix Coyotes 3-2 at Joe Louis Arena.

Feb. 18 Suffered a sprained right knee in a game against the Colorado Avalanche and missed six games.

Apr. 6 Scoring twice against goalie Nikolai Khabibulin in a 4-1 win over the Chicago Blackhawks at Joe Louis Arena, Lidstrom finished the season with 70 points, which led all NHL defensemen.

Apr. 10 Appeared in his 16th consecutive Stanley Cup playoffs, as Detroit opened the post-season with a 3-1 victory over the Nashville Predators at Joe Louis Arena, shattering Steve Yzerman's team mark.

Apr. 18 Played his 197th Stanley Cup game as Detroit downed the Nashville Predators 2-1 at Joe Louis Arena, surpassing Steve Yzerman's club record.

Apr. 22 Announced as a finalist for the Norris Trophy.

Apr. 29 Played his 201st Stanley Cup game as Detroit defeated the Colorado Avalanche 4-3, surpassing Jari Kurri for the most playoff games played by a European NHLer.

June 4 Won his fourth Stanley Cup as Detroit downed the Pittsburgh Penguins 3-2 at Mellon Arena, becoming the first European-born and trained captain of a Stanley Cup winner in NHL history.

June 9 Lidstrom and Wings goalier Chris Osgood appear with the Stanley Cup on 'The Tonight Show with Jay Leno'.

June 12 Awarded the Norris Trophy as the NHL's best defenseman for the sixth time in seven seasons.

Sept. 24 Suffered a broken nose when hit in the face with a puck during a pre-season game against the Montreal Canadiens at Joe Louis Arena. Lidstrom donned a visor when he returned to action.

Oct. 14 When the Stanley Cup champion Red Wings are invited to the White House, Lidstrom hands over two Detroit jerseys – No. 43 to U.S. President George W. Bush, and No. 41 to his dad, George H.W. Bush, representing the terms they served.

Dec. 4 Scored a goal and assisted on two others in a 6-5 win over the Vancouver Canucks at Joe Louis Arena.

Dec. 10 Scored 3:50 into overtime as Detroit rallied from a 3-1 deficit to beat the Calgary Flames 4-3 at Joe Louis Arena.

Dec. 20 Collected three assists during a 6-4 victory over the Los Angeles Kings at Joe Louis Arena.

Dec. 27 Missed two games due to an ankle injury.

2009

Jan. 6 Added to Western Conference roster for Jan. 25 NHL All-Star Game at Montreal's Bell Centre.

Jan. 20 Scored twice in a 6-3 loss to the Phoenix Coyotes at Jobing.com Arena.

Jan. 21 Opted out of the NHL All-Star Game to rest his injured ankle.

Jan. 23 Suspended by NHL for one game for opting out of NHL All-Star Game.

Feb. 4 Scored the game-winning goal on goalie Ilya Bryzgalov with 38 seconds left in regulation time in a 5-4 victory over the Phoenix Coyotes at Joe Louis Arena in his 1,300th NHL game.

Playoff Arenas Played In

Arena (Team)	GP	G	A	PTS	PIM
Honda Center (Anaheim)*	12	1	8	9	6
Pengrowth Saddledome (Calgary)	6	0	2	2	6
Raleigh Entertainment and Sports Center (Carolina)	2	0	0	0	0
Chicago Stadium (Chicago)	2	0	1	1	0
United Center (Chicago)	3	1	2	3	0
McNichols Arena (Colorado)	9	3	6	9	2
Pepsi Center (Colorado)	8	0	5	5	4
Nationwide Arena (Columbus)	2	1	1	2	0
Reunion Arena (Dallas)	5	0	4	4	2
American Airlines Arena (Dallas)	3	0	1	1	2
Joe Louis Arena (Detroit)	135	31	73	104	36
Rexall Place (Edmonton)	3	1	1	2	2
STAPLES Center (Los Angeles)	5	1	4	5	0
Metropolitan Sports Center (Minnesota)	3	1	0	1	0
Bridgestone Arena (Nashville)**	9	1	0	1	2
Meadowlands Arena (New Jersey)	2	0	1	1	0
CoreStates Spectrum (Philadelphia)	2	0	0	0	0
America West Arena (Phoenix)	3	1	4	5	2
Jobing.com Arena (Phoenix)	6	3	2	5	0
Mellon Arena (Pittsburgh)	6	1	2	3	0
Savvis Center (St. Louis)***	11	1	6	7	4
HP Pavilion (San Jose)****	15	5	3	8	6
Maple Leaf Gardens (Toronto)	3	0	0	0	0
GM Place (Vancouver)	3	2	0	2	0
MCI Center (Washington)	2	0	0	0	0
Winnipeg Arena (Winnipeg)	3	0	3	3	2
TOTALS	**263**	**54**	**129**	**183**	**76**

*-Also known as Arrowhead Pond (1993-94 to 2005-06).
**-Also known as Nashville Arena (1998-99; 2005-06 to 2006-07; 2009-10), Gaylord Entertainment Center (1999-2000 to 2004-05) and Sommet Center (2007-08 to 2009-10).
***-Also known as Kiel Center (1994-95 to 1999-2000).
****-Also known as San Jose Arena (1993-04 to 2000-01) and Compaq Center (2001-02).

TIMELINE

2009 continued

Feb. 18	Scored twice and drew an assist as Detroit downed the Nashville Predators 6-2 at Joe Louis Arena.
Mar. 12	Scored a goal and picked up two assists in a 6-5 shootout win over the Calgary Flames at Joe Louis Arena.
Apr. 2	Scored once and picked up two assists in a 5-4 loss to the St. Louis Blues at Joe Louis Arena.
Apr. 23	Announced as a finalist for the Norris Trophy.
May 2	Scored his second goal of the game with 49.1 seconds left in regulation time to give the Wings a 3-2 victory over the Anaheim Ducks in Game 1 of their Stanley Cup Western Conference semifinals series. Also assisted on Detroit's third goal.
May 19	Collected his 116th Stanley Cup assist on a goal by Brian Rafalski in a 3-2 victory over the Chicago Blackhawks in Game 2 of the Western Conference finals, surpassing Steve Yzerman to become Detroit's all-time leader.
May 24	Missed two playoff games due to a lower-body injury, ending his consecutive Stanley Cup games played streak at 228.
June 18	Finished third in Norris Trophy voting. Named to NHL Second All-Star Team.
Aug. 27	Named to Swedish preliminary roster for 2010 Winter Olympic Games in Vancouver.
Sept. 24	Named NHL player of the decade by The Sporting News.
Sept. 29	Named Ambassador of Honor for his home county of Dalarna, Sweden.
Oct. 2-3	The Red Wings open the NHL season with back-to-back games against the St. Louis Blues in Lidstrom's home country of Sweden.
Oct. 15	An assist on a Henrik Zetterberg goal during a 5-2 over the Los Angeles Kings at Joe Louis Arena makes Lidstrom the eighth defenseman in NHL history to record 1,000 career points and the first from Europe.
Oct. 20	Appointed along with Chris Chelios, Mark Recchi and Rob Blake as part of a committee designated to study and restructure the operations of the NHLPA.
Nov. 14	Honored by the NHL for reaching the 1,000-point plateau prior to Detroit's game at Joe Louis Arena against the Anaheim Ducks.
Dec. 14	Named NHL player of the decade by Sports Illustrated.
Dec. 23	Appeared in a music video of the song "That's What Christmas Means to Me" with Alyonka and Diana Larionov, daughters of Lidstrom's former teammate Igor Larionov, to benefit Hockey Fights Cancer.
Dec. 26	Named captain of Team Sweden for the 2010 Winter Olympic Games in Vancouver.
Dec. 26	Assisted on both goals in a 2-1 victory over the Columbus Blue Jackets at Joe Louis Arena as Lidstrom played his 1,373rd NHL game, surpassing Teppo Numminen for the most games played by a European player.
Dec. 27	Named to the All-Decade Team by NHL.com.

2010

Jan. 26	Scored twice in a 5-4 overtime loss to the Phoenix Coyotes at Joe Louis Arena.
Feb. 15-24	Played for Sweden in the Vancouver Winter Olympic Games.
Feb. 22	Honored with other members of the Triple Gold Club — winners of the Stanley Cup, Olympic gold medal and IIHF World Championships — at Hockey Canada House during Vancouver Winter Olympic Games.
Mar. 5	Recorded his 800th NHL assist on a goal by Tomas Holmstrom during a 5-2 win over Nashville Predators at Joe Louis Arena.
Mar. 19	Became the 31st player in NHL history to play 1,400 games in a 3-2

Milestone Goals

NO.	DATE	RESULT	ASSISTS	GOALTENDER
1	Oct. 17, 1991	St. Louis 3 at Detroit 6	Jimmy Carson and Steve Chiasson	Vincent Riendeau
100	March 26, 1999	Tampa Bay 1 at Detroit 6	Igor Larionov	Corey Schwab
189	April 15, 2006	Detroit 3 at St. Louis 2	Tomas Holmstrom and Henrik Zetterberg	Jason Bacashihua*
200	March 2, 2007	Chicago 2 at Detroit 6	Robert Lang and Pavel Datsyuk	Nikolai Khabibulin
264	March 26, 2012	Columbus 2 at Detroit 7	Henrik Zetterberg and Ian White	Steve Mason

Milestone Assists

NO.	DATE	RESULT	GOAL SCORER
1	Oct. 5, 1991	Detroit 5 at Toronto 8	Jimmy Carson
100	Dec. 14, 1993	Anaheim 2 at Detroit 5	Paul Coffey
200	Oct. 24, 1995	Ottawa 2 at Detroit 1	Paul Coffey
300	Jan. 16, 1999	Detroit 2 at Vancouver 2	Igor Larionov
383	Oct. 28, 2000	Columbus 1 at Detroit 4*	Darren McCarty
400	Dec. 31, 2000	Los Angeles 1 at Detroit 2	Steve Yzerman
500	Dec. 28, 2002	Detroit 4 at Nashville 2	Sergei Fedorov
600	March 7, 2006	Phoenix 5 at Detroit 2	Pavel Datsyuk
700	Jan. 2, 2008	Dallas 1 at Detroit 4	Pavel Datsyuk
800	March 5, 2010	Nashville 2 at Detroit 5	Tomas Holmstrom
878	March 28, 2012	Detroit 2 at Columbus 4	Niklas Kronwall

Milestone Points

NO.	DATE	RESULT	ASSISTS	GOAL/ASSIST
1	Oct. 5, 1991	Detroit 5 at Toronto 8	Jimmy Carson	Goal
100	April 1, 1993	Detroit 3 at Chicago 1	Steve Yzerman and Dino Ciccarelli	Goal
200	Nov. 17, 1995	Detroit 5 at Edmonton 4	Steve Yzerman	Goal
300	Feb. 29, 1996	New York 1 at Detroit 5	Dino Ciccarelli and Greg Johnson	Goal
400	Feb. 9, 1999	Detroit 5 at Nashville 2	Larry Murphy and Sergei Fedorov	Goal
500	Oct. 21, 2000	Buffalo 4 at Detroit 5	Brendan Shanahan	Goal
571	Oct. 12, 2001	Buffalo 2 at Detroit 4	Brendan Shanahan	Goal*
600	Jan. 25, 2002	Phoenix 1 at Detroit 4	Igor Larionov	Goal
700	Nov. 12, 2003	Detroit 6 at Dallas 2	Steve Yzerman	Goal
800	April 2, 2006	Detroit 3 at Minnesota 2	Robert Lang	Goal
900	Dec. 22, 2007	Detroit 4 at Minnesota 1	Daniel Cleary	Goal
1,000	Oct. 15, 2009	Los Angeles 2 at Detroit 5	Henrik Zetterberg	Goal
1,100	March 5, 2011	Detroit 4 at Phoenix 5	Valtteri Filppula	Goal
1,142	March 28, 2012	Detroit 2 at Columbus 4	Niklas Kronwall	Goal

TIMELINE

Apr. 27   A day prior to his 40th birthday, scored twice on goalie Ilya Bryzgalov and assisted on another goal as Detroit downed the Phoenix Coyotes 6-1 in Game 7 of their Stanley Cup opening-round series at Jobing.com Arena.

June 1   Agreed to a one-year contract to play his 19th season with the Red Wings.

June 13   Served as honorary pace car driver during the NASCAR Sprint Cup race at Michigan International Speedway.

June 23   Named to NHL Second All-Star Team.

Oct. 16-Nov. 13   Enjoyed a career high 11-game point-scoring streak.

Oct. 23   Collected three assists during a 5-4 win over the Anaheim Ducks at Joe Louis Arena.

Nov. 21   Assisted on two goals and scored the overtime winner as Detroit beat the Calgary Flames 5-4 at Joe Louis Arena.

Dec. 15   Beat goalie Jaroslav Halak twice and added a third goal into an empty net during a 5-2 win over the St. Louis Blues to join Mathieu Schneider and Reed Larson as the only Red Wings defensemen to record a hat-trick. Also picked up an assist to equal his career high for points in a game and became the oldest NHL defenseman to record a three-goal game.

Dec. 27   Scored once and assisted on three goals to tie his career high for points in a game during a 4-3 overtime victory over the Colorado Avalanche at the Pepsi Center.

2011

Jan. 10   Named to the roster for the Jan. 30 NHL All-Star Game at Carolina's RBC Center.

Jan. 18   Voted the captain of Team Lidstrom for the Jan. 30 NHL All-Star Game at Carolina's RBC Center. Team captains were voted on by the other players slated to participate in the game.

Jan. 30   Recorded an assist and was plus-7 as Team Lidstrom edged Team Staal 11-10 in the NHL All-Star Game at Carolina's RBC Center.

Mar. 5   Recorded a pair of assists in a 5-4 shootout loss to the Phoenix Coyotes at Jobing.com Arena to reach the 1,100 point plateau.

Mar. 24   The road leading up to the Novi Ice Arena was renamed Nick Lidstrom Drive. Lidstrom resided in Novi during his Red Wings career and his sons played youth hockey there.

Mar. 28   With a goal against Chicago goalie Corey Crawford in a 3-2 overtime loss to the Blackhawks at Joe Louis Arena, Lidstrom, 40, became the oldest NHL defenseman to record a 60-point season.

Apr. 13   When he took the ice for his shift of Detroit's 4-2 victory over the Phoenix Coyotes at Joe Louis Arena in Game 1 of their opening-round playoff series, Lidstrom appeared in his 248th Stanley Cup game, surpassing Patrick Roy for second on the all-time list.

Apr. 16   With two assists in a 4-2 win over the Phoenix Coyotes in Game 2 of their opening-round Stanley Cup series at Joe Louis Arena, Lidstrom improved to plus-55, surpassing Peter Forsberg (plus-54) as the all-time leader in Stanley Cup history.

Apr. 21   Announced as a finalist for the Lady Byng Trophy.

Apr. 24   Announced as a finalist for the Norris Trophy.

May 6   Scored twice on goalie Antti Niemi as Detroit downed the San Jose Sharks 4-3 in Game 4 of their Stanley Cup Western Conference semifinals series.

May 17   Named to The Sporting News NHL All-Star Team.

June 6   Nominated as a finalist for the Mark Messier Leadership Award.

June 19   Agreed to a one-year contract to play a 20th season with the Red Wings.

June 23   Won the Norris Trophy as NHL's best defenseman for the seventh time. At

TEAM LIDSTROM

Lidstrom Firsts

Most regular-season games played by a player born in Europe (1,564)

Most regular-season games played by a player in a career spent with only one team (1564)

Most regular-season games played by a player born in Sweden (1,564)

Most regular-season assists by a player born in Sweden (878)

Most regular-season wins played in (900)

Most career postseason games played with a single franchise (263)

Most career postseason assists by a defenseman born in Europe (129)

Most career postseason assists by a defenseman born in Sweden (129)

Most career postseason points by a defenseman with a single franchise (183)

Most career postseason points by a defenseman born in Europe (183)

Most career postseason points by a defenseman born in Sweden (183)

Most career postseason games played by a player born in Europe (263)

Most career postseason games played by a player born in Sweden (263)

Most career postseason assists by a defenseman with a single franchise (129)

Highest career postseason plus/minus (plus-61)

Most career postseason power-play goals by a defensemen (30)

Most career postseason shots on goal with single franchise (656)

Oldest player to record his first hat trick (40 years, 210 days)

Oldest defenseman to record a hat trick (40 years, 210 days)

Oldest Norris Trophy winner (41 years, 57 days in 2010–2011)

Most Consecutive Years in the Stanley Cup playoffs (20)**

**Shared with Larry Robinson

Lidstrom Firsts

First European-born and trained Norris Trophy winner (2000–01)

First European-born and trained Conn Smythe Trophy winner (2001–02)

First European-born and trained captain of a Stanley Cup-winning team (2008)

First European-born and trained defenseman to reach 1,000 points

First European-born and trained defenseman in NHL to win James Norris Memorial Trophy three years running (2001–2003, 2006–2008)

2011 continued

Sept. 8 — Named the NHL's best defenseman by the Hockey News.

Oct. 22 — Collected an assist on a Niklas Kronwall goal in a 7-1 loss to the Washington Capitals at the Verizon Center as Lidstrom became the 14th NHLer to play 1,500 games.

Nov. 5 — Scored twice and assisted on another goal as Detroit blanked the Anaheim Ducks 5-0 at Joe Louis Arena.

Nov. 11 — Detroit's 3-0 victory over the Edmonton Oilers makes Lidstrom the first player in NHL history to play in 900 regular-season victories by his team.

2012

Jan. 16 — Scored a goal as Detroit won a club-record 15th straight home game, defeating the Buffalo Sabres 5-0 at Joe Louis Arena.

Jan. 25 — Missed Detroit's 7-2 loss to the Montreal Canadiens at the Bell Centre due to stomach flu, ending his consecutive games streak at 213.

Jan. 27 — Lidstrom is featured in NBC's 'NHL 36' program.

Feb. 12 — Played his 1,550th game as a Red Wing, shattering former Detroit captain Alex Delvecchio's NHL mark for most games played with one team, in a 4-3 victory over the Philadelphia Flyers at Joe Louis Arena.

Feb. 14 — Drew an assist as the Red Wings set the NHL record with their 21st straight home-ice win, a 3-1 victory over the Dallas Stars at Joe Louis Arena.

Feb. 19 — Named the NHL's best role model in a poll of NHL players conducted by the NHLPA.

Feb. 28-Mar. 21 — Missed a career-high 11 games due to an ankle injury.

Mar. 26 — Scored his last goal as a Red Wing in a 7-2 victory over the Columbus Blue Jackets at Joe Louis Arena.

Mar. 28 — Collected his final assist as a Red Wing on a goal by Niklas Kronwall in a 4-2 loss to the Columbus Blue Jackets at Nationwide Arena.

May 31 — Announced his retirement as an NHL player.

July 8 — Hired as a scout by the Red Wings.

2013

May 3-19 — Served as an ambassador during the IIHF World Hockey Championship in Stockholm.

2014

Feb. 28 — He is inducted into the Michigan Sports Hall of Fame during a ceremony at the historic Max M. Fisher Music Center in Detroit. Other inductees in the Class of 2014 are broadcaster Jim Brandstatter; Detroit Lions Dorne Dibble and Jason Hanson; Michigan State football star Percy Snow; Atlanta Braves pitcher John Smoltz; U.S. soccer star Alexi Lalas; and Detroit Catholic Central football coach Tom Mach.

Mar. 6 — Lidstrom's No. 5 is retired prior to the Red Wings' game at Joe Louis Arena against the Colorado Avalanche.

May 25 — Lidstrom is among five players in the 18th class of the International Ice Hockey Federation Hall of Fame, which will be enshrined during a ceremony at the World Championship in Minsk, Belarus. Other inductees are former Red Wings Steve Yzerman and the late Ruslan Salei, as well as Soviet Union Olympic stars Vyacheslav Bykov and Andrei Khomutov.

Lidstrom Red Wings Records

CAREER

Most postseason goals by a defenseman (54)

Most postseason power-play goals (30)

Most power-play goals by a defenseman (132)

Most postseason points by a defenseman (183)

Most postseason assists (129)

Most postseason games played (263)

Most consecutive seasons in the postseason (20)

Most games played by a defenseman (1,564)

Most goals by a defenseman (264)

Most assists by a defenseman (878)

Most points by a defenseman, career (1,142)

Best postseason plus/minus, career (plus-61)

Best regular-season plus/minus, career (plus-450)

Most All-Star Game appearances by a defenseman (12)

SINGLE SEASON

Most points by a defenseman (80 in 2005-06)

Most assists by a defenseman (64 in 2005-06)

Most goals in a single postseason by a defenseman (six in 1998)***

Most points in a single postseason by a defenseman (19 in 1998)

Most assists by a rookie defenseman (49 in 1991-92)

Most points by a rookie defenseman (60 in 1991-92)****

Most assists by a rookie (49 in 1991-92)*****

*** *Shared with Paul Coffey*   **** *Shared with Reed Larson*   ***** *Shared with Marcel Dionne*

SINGLE GAME

Most assists in one postseason game (four on April 21, 2007)******

****** *Shared with Eddie Bush, Earl (Dutch) Reibel, Sergei Fedorov, Chris Chelios, and Todd Bertuzzi*

Most assists in one postseason game by a defenseman (four on April 21, 2007)******

****** *Shared with Eddie Bush and Chris Chelios*

DETROIT RED WINGS
LEGENDS

LIDSTROM

5

1991-2012

NUMBER RETIRED

March 6, 1994

SAWCHUK

1

1949-1955

1957-1964   1968-1969

NUMBER RETIRED
November 10, 1991

LINDSAY

7

1944-1957

HOWE

9

1946-1971

DELVECCHIO

10

1950-1974

ABEL

12

1938-1943

YZERMAN

19

1983-2006